REWRITE
YOUR
LIFE

Praise for
Rewrite Your Life

"My favorite kind of self-help book: irreverent, personal, and superbly useful."

—JEN MANN, *New York Times* best-selling author of *People I Want to Punch in the Throat*

"A lively exploration of writing's therapeutic value and an encouraging invitation to apply it to your life."

—KENDRA LEVIN, author of *The Hero is You*

"On occasion a gem of a book comes along. One that sticks with us and helps us to remember, we can rewrite our life. That our journey is filled with plot twists we never expected and that we can gain insights and perspective by exploring those unexpected events, or 'story food' through writing. *Rewrite Your Life* is just such a book. You will walk away with an understanding of how to heal through writing fiction and have the tools you need to make a difference in your own life and everyone your life touches."

—LYSSA DANEHY DEHART, MSW, LICSW, PCC, author of the blog *StoryJacking*

"Part how-to, part memoir, part so-funny-that-reading-it-in-public-was-difficult-without-disturbing-others, this is a book to give anyone who wants to be a writer, or a better one, anyone who thinks they have a story to tell. Which is everyone. Buy this book for everyone. Except me, I already have one and no, you can't borrow it."

—NORA MCINERNY PURMORT, author of *It's Okay to Laugh: (Crying Is Cool Too)* and host of the "Terrible, Thanks for Asking" APM podcast

REWRITE YOUR LIFE

Discover Your Truth
Through the Healing Power of Fiction

JESSICA LOUREY

Conari Press

Cover Design: Jim Warner
Cover Art: watercolor © Taira / shutterstock
Setting the Circle diagram concept created by Tony Van Den Einde
Layout Design: Kate Kaminski, Happenstance Type-O-Rama

For permission requests, please contact the publisher at:
Mango Publishing Group
2850 S Douglas Road, 2nd Floor
Coral Gables, FL 33134 USA
info@mango.bz

For special orders, quantity sales, course adoptions and corporate sales, please
email the publisher at sales@mango.bz. For trade and wholesale sales, please
contact Ingram Publisher Services at customer.service@ingramcontent.com or
+1.800.509.4887.

Rewrite Your Life: Discover Your Truth Through the Healing Power of Fiction

Library of Congress Cataloging-in-Publication Data available upon request
ISBN: 978-1-57324-693-4
BISAC category code LAN002000, LANGUAGE ARTS & DISCIPLINES /
Writing / Authorship

Printed in the United States of America

To Rex Veeder, who encouraged this.
I am forever grateful.

Contents

Introduction

TRUTH IN FICTION

Tell all the Truth but tell it slant —
Success in Circuit lies
Too bright for our infirm Delight
The Truth's superb surprise
As Lightning to the Children eased
With explanation kind
The Truth must dazzle gradually
Or every man be blind —
                    —Emily Dickinson

On September 13, 2001, I stood in front of my multicultural lit class assigning a response essay. The class was small, five students, all enrolled in my Technical Communication program. Because I taught all but one of their courses, we'd become a sort of tribe. I remember being excited about the assignment. I don't remember what I was wearing. I do remember I was growing my hair out and that I was worried about the pregnancy weight I was putting on and whether or not something I'd elected to call "Bonus Lunch" was doing me any favors. I remember being tired. It was a Thursday.

The door opened, and the college's office administrator stepped into my classroom. It was a first. She was unable to meet my eyes.

"Can you please come to the Dean's office?"

"Yup." I grabbed my briefcase. I knew I wasn't coming back.

Our final conversation thirty-six hours earlier had ended exactly like this:

HIM: *You're beautiful.*

ME: Silence.

HIM: *I love you.*

ME: *I don't think that means the same thing to you as it does to me.*

We'd been married for twenty-four days. I was three months pregnant. We'd timed it so that I could have the summer off after the baby was born, not expecting that we'd nail it on our first try. The University of Minnesota conference I'd been driving to that morning had been unexpectedly canceled as college campuses all over the country shut down. America was under attack, we were told.

I returned home to find something I hadn't expected to find.

# # #

There were two plainclothes detectives sitting in the Dean's office. They rose when we entered. The office administrator disappeared. I was with strangers.

"Is my daughter all right?" The question was a morbid courtesy in that overexposed moment, an invitation for the detectives to deliver good news before they leveled my world. My baby girl was three, and it was naptime in the day care across the street. I knew she was fine because I would have known if she wasn't.

I also knew that my husband had killed himself.

I had known I would be here, or somewhere like here, since the fist of blackbirds had dived at my car as I'd returned from the canceled U of M conference two days earlier. It was the blackbirds' warning that had forced me online to search his history, the coldness of their black bodies blocking out the sun that had warned me my life was never going to be the same again.

But I couldn't have known.

He was not depressed. He was a successful Department of Natural Resources ecologist with a family who loved him. Tall, dark-eyed, with a contagious smile and a meticulous work ethic, he baked pies for hospice care fundraisers and coached the local youth soccer league. We were newlyweds with a baby on the way. And so I took the chair the detectives offered, and I watched their faces, and I felt every corner of me shut down except my eyes and my ears. These organs became disconnected recording devices, and so while I can recall the entire conversation, it doesn't mean any more now than it did then. Just words.

"Do you know where your husband is?"

"Um, we had a fight two days ago. He drove to his old house, the one we have on the market? I haven't heard from him since."

They exchanged glances. Their suits were immaculate. Both men looked like what I imagined New York detectives look like, polished as stones. The detective who drew the short straw adjusted his collar. "Your husband killed himself."

I felt the baby kick, or did I just feel kicked? "When?"

"He was found today, by a coworker. There was a murder-suicide in the same DNR office two years ago, and they were worried for you and your daughter."

"He killed himself today?"

"He was found today."

This was important. If he killed himself immediately after our argument, that meant I'd been thinking about a dead man, emailing a corpse, for two days. But I already knew the truth of that, too.

His ghost had visited me the first night.

# # #

Mysteries involve murder. They can also include sex, humor, and intrigue, but if it's a grown-up mystery, readers are going to expect a body, preferably in Chapter 1. I knew this. Everybody knows this. Mysteries are also formulaic, another widely accepted belief.

What I didn't realize until my husband's suicide was that mysteries are also, at their simplest, about plumbing human motivation and creating closure. I found myself suddenly, urgently, needing both. A friend had lent me a Sue Grafton alphabet mystery a couple years earlier. I read it, and then I went to the library and checked out more. After I devoured all of them, I turned to Tony Hillerman. Then Janet Evanovich. William Kent Krueger. I was greedy, always a fast reader, stuffing one into my head, then another, and another.

Each novel pulled dark secrets into the light.

Each story ended with The Answers.

# # #

The United States is a pop psychology culture. We know the five stages of grief and that alcoholism is a disease, that communication is key, that men are from Mars and women from Venus. Here are things, however, that they don't tell you about suicide:

1. If you hear your husband's final words, and they come after he has made up his mind to end his life, you will forever be able to replay them in your head in Dolby surround sound. This is because there is an audible click that happens when a living man begins to speak as a dead man, and a dead man's voice is terrifying.

2. The police officer working the case will mean well, but he still has to ask you if you want to take home the gun your husband shot himself with. If the officer is also new to the force, he may wonder aloud, with a mixture of awe and revulsion, how a person could choose a muzzle-loading rifle to do the deed. Finally, if he is both new to the force and young, he may hand you your husband's glasses without noticing that they have tiny fragments of gray and red matter on them.

3. The phlebotomist taking your blood may not consider what brought you into her lab or guess that after six agonizing weeks, you've finally decided to remove your wedding ring. She will

only see a pregnant, single woman getting an HIV test, and you will disgust her.

4. Trying to get a handle on grief without answers is like trying to snap a photograph of the whole world while you're standing on it.

#

Three months after Jay shot himself, I was heading to the basement to do laundry. I stepped off the bottom step into a puddle of dog pee, slipped, and landed on my back without any mediating flailing, just *smack*, ridiculously pregnant lady flat on the linoleum-covered cement, soaking up cold urine and staring at the ceiling. Maybe my head hit first because I couldn't decide what to do next. In fact, I remember feeling profoundly relaxed, removed from everything, just right, *oh, yes, I could stay here forever.*

Zoë skipped out of her playroom. Using a beautiful logic unique to three-year-olds (*Mommy is playing lay down!*), she was delighted rather than alarmed to find me sprawled out. She plopped down cross-legged near my head and wiggled her body underneath me. Now the dog pee was dripping from my hair onto her lap.

"We'll be okay, Mommy."

I'm not sure to this day what she meant by that. Probably she was only repeating what I said to her daily as a sort of prophylactic wish. She began to pet my head like I did for her when she was sick. As she stroked my pee hair, she hummed a song, equal parts "Happy Birthday" and "*Frère Jacques.*" The dog padded downstairs and curled next to me.

The three of us stayed like that until I remembered how to move. *We'll be okay, Mommy.*

#

I'd read twenty mysteries before I finally decided to write one. My belly was swollen. I could go an hour at a time without thinking of him. My brain and heart were starved. I lived at the end of a lonely country road that the plows visited last, and I saw how people were looking at me.

Pregnant. Husband killed himself. Out there alone with a three-year-old, forty miles from the nearest hospital.

People wanted to help. They worried about me. I still carry that with me, all their worry, all the pain they tried to haul for me so I wouldn't have to heft it alone. Not just my friends and family, but strangers reached out to hold me up, and they didn't stop even after the funeral. Grief is selfish, though, and so I could only watch and keep turning inward.

Writing a novel saved me.

# # #

Here's how *May Day*, the first mystery I wrote, begins:

I tried not to dwell on the fact that the only decent man in town had stood me up. Actually, he may have been the only literate, single man in a seventy-mile radius who was attracted to me and attractive. The warm buzz that was still between my legs tried to convince the dull murmur in my head that it was just a misunderstanding. To distract myself from thoughts of Jeff's laugh, mouth, and hands, I downed a couple aspirin for my potato chip hangover and began the one job I truly enjoyed at the library: putting away the books.

I glanced at the spines of the hardcovers in my hands and strolled over to the Pl-Sca aisle, thinking the only thing I really didn't like about the job was picking magazine inserts off the floor. Certainly the reader saw them fall, but without fail, gravity was too intense to allow retrieval except by a trained library staff member. I bet I found three a day. But as I teetered down the carpeted aisle in my flowered heels, I discovered a new thing not to like: there was a guy lying on the tight-weave Berber with his legs lockstep straight, his arms crossed over his chest, and a reference book opened on his face. He was wearing a familiar blue-checked shirt, and if he was who I thought he was, I knew him intimately. A sour citrus taste rose at the back of my throat. Alone, the library aisle wasn't strange; alone, the man wasn't strange. Together, they made my heart slam through my knees. I prodded his crossed legs with my foot and felt no warmth and no give.

My eyes scoured the library in a calm panic, and I was aware of my neck creaking on its hinges. I could smell only books and stillness, tinged with a faint coppery odor. Everything was in order except the dead man laid out neatly on the carpeting, wearing the same flannel I had seen him in two days earlier. I wondered chaotically if dead people could lie, if they still got to use verbs after they were gone, and if maybe this was the best excuse ever for missing a date. Then I had a full-body ice wash, five years all over again, a nightmare pinning me to my bed as I silently mouthed the word "mom."

Had proximity to me killed him?

# # #

Six months after Jay's suicide, I called my mom and asked if she'd stay overnight at my house. She had driven the two hours one way to sleep over every Monday since his death, but this was a Thursday. My dad visited when I asked, was over regularly to repaint walls and fix leaks, but he preferred his own bed and had never slept in my house. He asked if he could come with mom that day, though. I said sure, I needed him to help carry some wood for the woodstove.

My water broke that night, with my parents sleeping upstairs in the spare bedroom and my daughter tucked safely in her room. I wasn't yet having contractions, but I rang the hospital to let them know that I'd be arriving soon. I'd called the hospital at least three times before to make advance arrangements for my daughter's birth and then my son's. Each time, different people, always female, answered the same impersonal way: "Douglas County Hospital, how may I direct your call?"

This time, the person on the other end of the line was a man. "This is Jay. How can I help you?"

Jay. My husband's name. I gripped the phone.

"Hello? Is someone there?"

"I'm having a baby." It came out a whisper.

"Fantastic!" He sounded so excited that I surprised myself by smiling. "Has your water broken?"

"Just now."

"First baby?"

"Second."

"Why don't you come in now? We'll take care of you."

My dad stayed with my daughter so she could sleep through the night. My mom drove me to Alexandria, steering her Ford Taurus between a moonscape of snowdrifts and the kind of cold that freezes the wet of your eyes. When we arrived, Jay took care of everything, just as he'd promised. My son, Xander, was born healthy and looking exactly like his dad. I had planned a big-sister party at the hospital, so Zoë arrived to balloons, presents, and cake, all for her. She surveyed the bounty and declared that having a little brother wasn't half bad.

# # #

I've never written about the facts of my husband's suicide before the words that you just read, but if you know my story, you can find it in every novel I write. My anxieties work themselves out in each book. I still hear his voice, I still fear the betrayal and loss that are around every corner, but I get to write the story, and at the end, the mystery is always solved. This is a slant way to deal with loss, but it's the only way I can do it. Only fiction offers me the truth.

What I have come to call "rewriting my life" didn't provide a clear, straight path from trauma to vibrant mental health and a two-book publishing contract. I was no pretty flower busting out of the crack in the pavement against all odds. The process was and continues to be a messy, three-steps-forward, two-and-a-half-steps-back kind of deal. But Jay's suicide put me at a crossroads where I could choose one of two life paths, drinking or writing, and I chose writing, thank god. Turns out rewriting your life works better than gin, which can only offer you empty calories and a holy calling to watch the entire season of *Looking for Love: Bachelorettes in Alaska*. (I researched it so you don't have to.) Crafting a novel, on the other hand, spins your pain, shame, and joy into gold, emotionally and literally.

I know you either are playing with the idea of writing a novel, or have already written one and want to take your fiction writing to the next level; otherwise, you wouldn't be reading this book. You're in good company. According to a study conducted by the Jenkins Group, 81 percent of Americans believe they have a book in them, and 27 percent of those want that book to be fiction. That's over seventy million people who want to write a great novel but aren't sure how. *Rewrite Your Life* walks you through the process of transforming what you know—your life experiences—into a powerful work of fiction, and subsequently transforming yourself.

I do have a request, though. As you read *Rewrite Your Life*, please don't equate the process of turning your life challenges into a novel with trying out for the Trauma Olympics. You don't win the gold the more pain you've experienced, though I think we all sometimes secretly believe that.

Pain is pain. Bad is bad; good is better.

Seriously, sometimes I'm sad or angry for no discernible reason. It counts.

If you still believe you need a pass to enter the writing club, I offer you this: transgenerational epigenetics strongly suggests that a sense of trauma can be passed down to you from your ancestors up to four generations back. That means if Great-Grandma Esther had a rough time of it, you can feel emotionally sapped even if your life is relatively good.

Besides, we all have different definitions of a "challenging experience." The point is to learn how to recycle your facts into fiction so you can experience the personal transformation that comes with rewriting your life. The novel you will craft will function as both your lighthouse and the Viking funeral boat upon which you get to burn your garbage once and for all.

An added bonus? At the end of this adventure, you will have a powerful novel inspired by your life, cooked of the same ingredients but wholly different.

By the way, while the instructions in this book work equally well for short stories, I consistently use the term "novel," because writing short stories has always reminded me of carving Mona Lisa on a grain of rice. If short stories speak to you more kindly than they do me, simply replace "novel" with "short story" in everything you read from this point forward. *Rewrite Your Life* offers you a road map for using your own life experiences, however fresh or ancient, deep or temporary, painful or proud they are, to craft a lush, powerful piece of fiction, regardless of that fiction's length.

One more thing. You don't need to be a gifted writer to rewrite your life. If you have something to write with or on, you're golden. I guarantee you're going to surprise yourself with what you create, on paper, inside yourself, and in the world.

So come on. Pack what you need. We're in this together.

Orientation

Throughout this book, you are asked to explore your history with a goal of translating it into healing, compelling fiction. Think of this process as a pilgrimage to your best future, an adventure that paradoxically requires you to travel through your past. Each chapter is full of examples, insight, and activities that will lead you through a purposeful excavation of your memories, showing you how to turn them into something greater than their individual parts, something healing and transformative. To that end, look for modest writing goals in each section that when added together result in a magnificent achievement: a healing novel inspired by your life experiences. See these helpful markers to guide you in best using this book as well as a packing list for this road trip of a lifetime.

MARKERS

Look for these icons to guide your odyssey.

 The Mile Marker symbol indicates a focused opportunity to unearth and repurpose a life experience. Have a paper and pen handy.

 The Map icon signals that you will be required to map out a leg in your novel-writing journey. Plan on writing when you see one of these.

 When you spot the Navigate icon, look for a tip that relates what you're presently reading to information covered in a previous chapter.

Recommended Packing List

- Pen or pencil.
- Notebook. A cheap drugstore-style spiral bound is perfect. If you're going to write your book longhand, make sure the notebook is big enough to hold all your words. On the inside cover (or the front cover, if you're feeling ballsy), write "Novel in Progress." I recommend writing it with a magic marker, scented, maybe cinnamon or blueberry, to lock in the memory of this brave undertaking. Plan on carrying that notebook around with you until your novel is written. You'll need it when you least expect it.
- Computer. This isn't necessary, but if you plan to type your novel on a computer, you'll need that in addition to your notebook.
- If you've still got room, consider packing a sense of humor, too. Actually, screw that. *Pack humor.*

REWRITE
YOUR
LIFE

PART I

THE POWER OF
FICTIONALIZING
YOUR LIFE

CHAPTER 1

THE SCIENCE OF
WRITING TO HEAL

Writing fiction is the act of weaving a series of lies to arrive at a greater truth.

—*Khaled Hosseini*

All sorrows can be borne if you put them into a story.

—*Isak Dinesen*

"You should write a book."

Maybe, like me, you first heard this as you shared the story of your daycare lady locking you and your sister in the closet before letting her creepy grown son perform puppet shows for the rest of the kids. Or, perhaps someone suggested novel-writing-as-a-release after you mentioned how close you'd come to getting car-jacked when your sweet, animal-loving friend pulled her Toyota into an unlit parking lot so you could both stand vigil over a dead dog in New Orleans' Lower Ninth. I call these types of experiences "story food," the life occurrences so remarkable that you can't help telling other people about them.

Here's another possibility: maybe you've never shared your most intense experiences with anyone because you're private, or think no one would believe you, or simply and understandably don't want to relive those moments, even within the safety of words. Yet, some secret, scrappy part of you is whispering to get that story out. If that's the case, I'm telling you what others have told me.

You should write a book.

Sure, it's a pop-off answer to anyone who's had a traumatic or amazing or unbelievable experience, but it turns out there is science behind it.

Mountains of it.

A BRIEF HISTORY OF CREATIVE THERAPIES

The human need to creatively express ourselves can be traced back to the oldest-surviving painting, scratched into an Indonesian cave forty thousand years ago. (By the way, it says a lot about human priorities that the first plow wasn't invented until thirty thousand years later, a fact that makes me weirdly happy.) Visual art as expression expanded and flourished from there, producing Michelangelos and Picassos and Gentileschis, but it wasn't until 1939 that the therapeutic value of art was established. That year found WWI veteran and artist Adrian Hill recovering from tuberculosis in a British sanatorium. While there, he was asked to teach painting classes to his fellow patients, many of them returning veterans and a lot of them assumedly bored. Hill witnessed firsthand art's healing power on those vets. He brought his discovery to the general public, coining the term "art therapy" in 1942.

Hill believed that the symbolic mediums of drawing and painting busied the hands and freed the mind, allowing the body's natural reparative mechanisms to do their work unimpeded. His hypothesis was oversimplified, but science would soon prove him right.

Writing as therapy began to catch up to art therapy in the 1960s when New York psychologist Dr. Ira Progoff introduced the concept of reflective writing for mental health. He called this process the Intensive Journal Method. As a Jungian, Dr. Progoff subscribed to the healing power of accessing unconscious or repressed memories. Like visual art therapists before him, he witnessed the therapeutic value of externalizing an emotion or experience, encapsulating it in an image or an essay and thereby releasing it.

Innovators Michael White, an Australian therapist, and Dr. James W. Pennebaker, an American social psychologist, built on Progoff's work in the 1980s. White, along with his colleague David Epston, established the narrative therapy movement. The movement's central tenet is that "the problem is the problem," not the person experiencing it, and that externalizing the problem by writing about it is the most effective way to address it. Dr. Pennebaker was a pioneer in the writing therapy, or expressive writing, movement, whose research into the connection between secrets, language, and mental health has been groundbreaking. Pennebaker was one of the first to clinically establish that basic writing exercises can significantly improve mental and physical health as well as work performance. His most famous book, *Opening Up: The Healing Power of Expressing Emotions*, accessibly demonstrates the connection between writing and healing.

HOW NARRATIVE THERAPY WORKS

Hundreds of studies have since been conducted to figure out how writing heals, because it *does* mend and transform. Social scientists have established that expressive writing decreases anxiety and depression; reduces pain and complex premenstrual symptoms; improves the body's immune functions including boosting antibody production; enhances working memory, physical performance, and social relationships; reduces illness-related doctor's visits; improves the physical and mental states of Alzheimer patients' caregivers, cancer patients, and people with HIV; reduces the symptoms of asthma, rheumatoid arthritis, and eating disorders; and positively addresses a host of PTSD symptoms. In fact, a recent pilot study of eleven veterans diagnosed with PTSD found that after a dozen sessions of narrative therapy, not only did over half of the veterans experience a clinically significant reduction of PTSD symptoms, but a quarter of them no longer met the criteria for PTSD.

That's just a start.

Writing makes everything better.

It's tied to how our brains are wired. We are creatures of habit, evolved animals who perceive stimuli, run it through our limbic system, attach significance to it, and then respond.

Stimulus—significance—response.

Here's an example. Let's say you're stuck in traffic. The traffic jam is a *stimulus*. It's the job of your amygdala, an almond-shaped glob of neurons housed deep in your brain, to process stimuli, organizing events into emotional memories. Your amygdala codes this particular experience with frustration, which is the *significance* you attach to it. You *respond* to this emotion by swearing and mentally squishing the heads of the people in the cars around you. This swearing and mental-head-squishing response becomes your established action pattern any time you perceive a stimulus that your amygdala has classified as frustrating.

Stimulus—significance—response.

Traffic jam—frustration—mental head squishing.

But you don't have to remain a slave to this feedback loop. Thanks to your evolved prefrontal cortex, the big chunk of brain directly behind your forehead that governs executive reasoning, you have the ability to break free of this stimulus-significance-response pattern. (Pavlov's dogs were not so lucky.) Still, as anyone who's tried to quit smoking knows, being aware of the best path and choosing it are two different beasts. And the more intense the emotion, the less blood flow to the prefrontal lobe, therefore the weaker our ability to make rational choices.

To add to the problem, it turns out your neural pathways cement themselves in the case of traumatic events. The result is that some people respond to *reminders* of stimuli, a condition known as post-traumatic stress disorder (PTSD). This trauma-induced reprogramming of the brain explains why it's impossible for many veterans to enjoy Fourth of July fireworks, for example. Their limbic system, the creamy nougat center of the human brain where our memories and emotional lives are housed, has coded "explosion" with "danger," and so when these veterans hear fireworks, they react as they would, as any of us would, to a bomb going off nearby.

From the outside, this condition may appear simple to correct. They're fireworks, not bombs, after all. But neuroimaging proves that when people are merely reminded of trauma, blood flow ramps up in the brain structures associated with extreme emotions and decreases in the areas associated with communication. The sufferer essentially becomes trapped in their own fear, at the mercy of neural patterns. The good news is that writing therapy, along with other mindfulness practices, including dialectical behavior therapy, art therapy, yoga, Qigong, tai chi, Alexander Technique, and meditation, allows you to reprogram your brain.

You can literally *change your mind*.

Drawing on the wide body of research in this area, the three most promising explanations as to how this works are habituation, catharsis, and inhibition-confrontation. I explain all three below.

Habituation

The effectiveness of habituation (note that the root word is "habit") in changing negative patterns is based on the fact that central nervous system arousal decreases with repeated exposure to a single stimulus. In other words, the familiar becomes boring.

Let me give you an example. Say you show up to your office job next Monday, thinking it's just another day. When you get to work, however, you discover a red-nosed clown sitting in your spare office chair, smiling opaquely at you, his red clown feet so huge that they disappear under your desk.

That would be frickin' *terrifying*.

You would call people. They would tell you not to worry, that the clown is there as some sort of cost-saving, effectiveness-lacking productivity exercise. You believe them, but Creepy the Clown is still horrifying, particularly because that empty smile remains stapled to his face as he silently watches you type.

Day two he's still there, he'd maybe be a *little* less freaky, but for sure you keep one eye pinned on him at all times. On day three, because he hasn't killed you yet, you decide maybe it's safe to move both eyes to your computer screen, at least when checking email. Come day four, you're in the middle of texting your friend a photo you've just taken of the front of your shirt, and more specifically the toothpaste smear shaped like a famous singer (#ifoundmintyelvis), before you remember that Creepy the Clown is sitting five feet away.

You see where this is going?

By the end of the week, you're all *meh*. He's a clown in a chair and you've crap to do.

You have become *habituated* to the clown.

Like all good programming, habituation has a genetic advantage. If we respond to something that is proven safe with a heightened nervous system, we don't have as much attention to give to what is *actually* dangerous. Now that we're walking upright, we can use this power of habituation to our advantage. Specifically, by writing about past stressful or traumatic situations, we can gain mastery over them, freeing up room to worry about the actual threats, which are far rarer than our ancient limbic systems would have us believe.

Catharsis

At its most basic, a catharsis is an emotional release or a cleansing. You've likely felt catharsis after confessing to a professional or venting to a friend. My first memory of catharsis came when I was seven. My family had moved from a medium-sized city to the small town of Paynesville, Minnesota, right before I began second grade. I had to hit the ground running. New school, new kids, new rules, and I was the kid wearing homemade jeans and garage sale tennis shoes with teeth stained gray due to an antibiotic I was injected with as an infant. As a scraggly bonus, I fiercely refused to comb any part of my hair that I couldn't directly see, which meant that whoever sat behind me got a real treat.

Suffice it to say, I was not fitting in.

That first day on the playground, three girls, their names mercifully lost to time, cornered me by the slide. The one with rainbow barrettes spoke for them all. "Where you from?"

Probably she was only curious. Maybe she was trying to be my friend. For sure, I blew it.

"St. Cloud. My dad's an actor on TV."

That's what's called a BIG FAT LIE. My dad had just quit his job as a cartographer to make a go at his dream of being a full-time alcoholic. What black alley that lie lurched out of, I'll never know.

"No way!"

"I swear on my mom's life." The air rushed out of me as soon as I said it. *Whoof.* Like I'd punched myself in the stomach. My mom was *everything* to me—security, safety, food, love, my oasis in a hurricane of a home life—and I'd just lied her life away. Talk about following the shit with the shovel.

You better believe the girls wanted to play with me after that. *Everyone wanted to play with me.* I should have been thrilled, but I was sick at what I'd done. I spent the rest of the day weeping in the nurse's office. When she offered to call my mom to come pick me up, I demurred, positive that if my mom wasn't already dead, she'd certainly croak on the drive in.

At the end of the day, I could barely drag myself off the bus and into the house. Against all odds, my mom was there, dead lady walking. She took one look at me before bundling me inside a hug.

"What's wrong?"

I rolled over on myself like a professional narc.

And you know what? I felt a thousand pounds lighter, imminent punishment for lying notwithstanding. I'd been hauling that weight all day. It felt great to lay it down.

Catharsis really can be that immediate and that effective. Think of cathartic sharing as removing the lid from a bubbling pot, where the steam is any extreme emotion—guilt, fear, anger—that has been bottled up. Engaging a negative experience by talking or writing about it, or a version of it, releases the more intense emotions associated with it. Catharsis "lets off steam."

Inhibition-Confrontation

According to inhibition-confrontation, the third theory of why writing is an effective pathway to emotional healing, it's hard work to avoid thinking about stress or trauma. This is the *inhibition* part of the name. Somehow, someway, the negative thoughts and impulses leak in despite our best efforts to tamp them down. This denial leads to chronic stress, which takes a toll on the mind and body.

Confronting these stressors through writing—the *confrontation* part of the name—produces immediate boosts in mental and physical well-being. The trauma or stress—in other words, the stimuli—still exists in memory form, but when you face it, its significance changes.

Here's an example. Think of your life ordeals as zombies trying to get in through your front door. You spend all your energy shoulder-to-the-door trying to keep them out—*inhibiting* the zombies' arrival—which doesn't leave much time or attention for anything else. Your very survival depends on keeping that door closed, but you're exhausted; you can only keep this up for so long, so you finally let down your guard. The zombies charge through, and—*what??*— you realize there were never any flesh-eating monsters on the other side of the door. It was *memories* of zombies you were holding back this whole time.

The arts, and specifically writing, provide a protected route for opening that door and letting the memories-masquerading-as-life-threats in. Once they're through, you free up all the time and energy you've spent shoring up that door. For my money, the most exciting part of this last theory is that what we've been inhibiting or holding doesn't need to be traumatic or long-buried. Through writing, we can confront even a minor annoyance and still reap health benefits.

In further good news, it isn't necessary to know which one of these three explanations you're tapping into to be sustained and healed by writing. You just need to write. You don't need to choose autobiography or memoir as your vehicle either, though both narrative therapy and expressive writing therapy are centered on factual writing, often in the forms of essays, journals, and letters.

What I have returned from the dark side to tell you is that fiction writing works just as well.

For some of us, it works even better.

REWRITING MY LIFE
THROUGH FICTION

In 1996, when nonfiction-specific writing therapy was gaining traction, Dr. Melanie A. Greenberg crafted a clever study in which she measured the curative properties of writing about a real traumatic experience, an imaginary traumatic experience, and a real neutral experience (the control group). Her findings? People writing about imaginary events were less depressed than people writing about actual trauma, and the fiction writers demonstrated significant physical health improvements. I liken this healing power of directed fiction writing to straight-up art therapy. You don't need to (and most of us probably aren't capable of) painting an exact representation of the issues you want to work through. Instead, you paint/sculpt/write/sketch an abstraction, and in the act of creation lies the cure.

The specific benefits of rewriting your life make even more sense when you consider Dr. Pennebaker's discovery that two elements above all else increase the therapeutic value of writing: creating a coherent narrative and shifting perspective. These are not coincidentally the cornerstones of short story and novel writing. Writers call them plot and point of view. And identical to expressive writing, the creation of fiction involves habituation, catharsis, and inhibition-confrontation, but from an emotionally safer perch than memoir. While I enjoy reading memoirs and wholly support anyone who wants to write them, and all of the healing benefits and many of the instructions in this book can be applied to this type of writing, writing memoir has never felt like a good fit for me. Writing fiction allows me to distance myself, to become a spectator to life's roughest seas. It gives form to our wandering thoughts, lends empathy to our perspective, allows us to cultivate compassion and wisdom by considering other people's motivations, and provides us practice in controlling attention, emotion, and outcome. We heal when we transmute the chaos of life into the structure of a novel, when we learn to walk through the world as observers and students rather than wounded, when we make choices about what parts of a story are important and what we can let go of.

I believe this in my core, but I knew none of this when Jay and I married. Back then, I hadn't heard of narrative or expressive writing therapy, and if I had, I'd have been put off by their focus on essay writing and memoir. I'd always enjoyed creative writing, though, had even crafted a rambling semblance of a novel as my master's thesis before I'd met Jay, a novel so awful that years later I tried to steal the only copy from the college library. (I was actually in the clear, thesis in hand outside the library, when guilt overtook me. In retrospect, bringing my then-ten-year-old son along was a mistake. The problem with raising your children right is that they're real wet blankets when it comes time to commit a crime.) After graduate school, though, I found myself newly married, teaching full-time, and pregnant with my second child. I barely had time for personal hygiene, let alone creativity.

Then, in the days and weeks following Jay's suicide, I couldn't imagine formulating a coherent sentence, let alone a book. Even landing in a cold puddle of dog pee wasn't enough to shift my grief into novel writing.

It took my deepest shame for me to learn to rewrite my life through fiction.

I'll try to type this without crying.

It was January, dead cold winter in northern Minnesota. Jay had been in the ground for exactly four months. The sharp loneliness that I wore like a shroud was all the more unsettling for the fact that I was carrying my son in my body—I felt like the unwilling meat in a death-and-life sandwich. I'd been shambling along, teaching a full load, parenting Zoë as well as I could. Life had become a numb routine: wake up, shower, drink coffee, get Zoë ready for day care, drive her there, teach, pick her up, drive her home, feed us, play, give her a bath, head to bed.

Wake up and repeat.

Something that still surprises me about grief is how much time you spend not feeling *anything*. You expect the crying jags and the pain so sharp you think you're having a heart attack. You can't prepare for the long stretches of feeling nothing, though, not curiosity, not joy, not even annoyance.

Nothing.

Four months into my full-time grief, I actually thought robot-me was doing pretty well, which shows the depths of my depression. My wake-up call came on January 15. Zoë was still three. She was also still stubborn, willful, and outspoken, like any respectable three-year-old, plus a little extra because she's always been my Princess Fury.

A blizzard had just roared through, and I knew the roads were gonna be tough. Plus, it was a new semester, so I had a whole slate of new classes, new students, new questions. Life felt extra heavy, a yoke on my shoulders and a person in my belly. And that feeling of *nothingness* was getting to me, a constant low buzzing that made it almost impossible to climb out of bed that morning.

But I did. I think it was muscle memory.

On this particular day, Zoë didn't want to go to day care, even more than usual. Yet, we went through the motions. In a numb haze, perched at the top of the basement stairs and near the garage door, I helped her with her pants. She flapped her legs like a wind-up doll the entire time. I tugged her shirt over her head. She screamed. I tried to yank her jacket on, and she went no-bones, melting onto the floor.

Then it came time to wrench on her boots.

One of her flailing legs connected with my face. *Smack.* The pain was raw and white and I snapped. Just like that, the force of the kick broke through my *nothing* and released pure black rage and something terrifyingly primal, a monster I didn't know I housed.

Here I need to take a break and tell you that my parents, for all their foibles and deep dysfunction, had never so much as yelled at me, forget spanking or hitting. I was raised to be an organic granola pacifist, someone whose go-to in times of conflict and stress has always been research followed by earnest communication. The idea of striking a child was as foreign and abhorrent to me as cutting off my own finger. Hitting *Zoë*, my baby fuzz, the tiny precious peanut I'd played music for while she was in my tummy, planned a water birth for to minimize her stress as she entered the world, nursed her whole first year despite a full-time job and a forty-minute commute each way so that I could directly deliver every nutrient she'd need to thrive?

Not on your life.

But dammit, I was gonna return that kick.

I was going to *smack her back.*

And I wasn't just going to hurt her. I was going to *punch her shut her up punish her make her hurt as bad as I did so help me it's survival to finally feel something because I am drowning in numbness and I can't go back to feeling nothing again so after I take care of her I'm going to—*

I can still taste the mustiness of the basement wafting up the stairs.

I can still see her red face, shock suffocating those beautiful green eyes.

She recognized, smelled it maybe, what I was about to do.

Hand still in the air, I fled. Like a woman morphing into a werewolf, I raced out of that house before I became a full monster who'd eat her own children.

The icy air wasn't enough to slap me back to my senses. I jumped into my car.

I started it.

I raced out of that driveway, the snowdrifts a sun-blocking wall of white on each side. My eyes were dry. Have you ever cut yourself so deep that it didn't bleed? That's what I'd done, cut too deep to even cry. I just drove, abandoning my wispy-haired, short-armed baby girl, the child who'd walked into her first day of Just for Kix, all belly and knees in her black leotard, clapped her hands to get everyone's attention, and in her high, precious voice thanked all the other little girls' parents for taking time out of their busy day to come watch her dance, the first true love of my life, Zoë Rayn.

I ran out on her because I feared what I would do if I stayed.

It took just past the end of the driveway for my prefrontal lobe to calm the animal in me. My daughter was three years old and alone in our house. I don't think she'd ever been alone in *a room* before. She was frightened of the dark and the entire basement, would grab my hand with her chubby fingers when strangers talked to her, was as defenseless as a newborn fawn.

My fear bowed to nausea. I tried to turn the car around, but the snow was too high, only a single lane plowed on my back country road. I had to drive one more icy mile before there was enough space to change direction, and by then, I was sobbing so hard that I was gagging. I'd seen the look of betrayal on her face in the forever-moment before I'd raced out of the house. It had been ringed with terror.

I pulled into the driveway and leapt out of the car without turning it off.

I'd been gone for six minutes, a lifetime to a three-year-old.

I raced into the house.

Zoë was exactly where I'd left her, on the floor, boots lying beside her.

Potty-trained for well over a year, she had wet herself in fear. The dark stain flowered on the front of her elastic-waisted jeans. A puddle had formed underneath her. She was staring at the ceiling, shuddering.

She'd seen that awful thing in my eyes, and then she'd heard me drive away.

I picked her up. I held her until she stopped shaking and the weeping came, that heaving gale of the shattered child. If my heart wasn't already broken, it would have cracked when she stuttered, "I'm sorry, Mommy. I'm sorry about my shoes."

I cried with her, told her she hadn't done anything wrong. I apologized, but I knew there would never be enough sorries. I cleaned her up, me up. I wanted to stay at home and hold her all day, shut out the world, but sometimes you catch a glimpse of unbending Truth and I knew that if I didn't step back into the stream of life that day, I wouldn't ever again.

I drove to day care. I confessed.

When I arrived at work, I called her dad, Lance, and told him, too, what I'd done. I'll never forget how kind he was in that phone call. I expected him to take her away from me, for day care to call the authorities. They would have been well within their rights. Instead, everyone supported me with that peculiar aching sadness, like they knew something I didn't.

I started writing *May Day* that night, after Zoë fell asleep.

Compiling journal entries wouldn't have worked for me. I couldn't survive reliving the pain, not then, not on my own. I needed to convert it, package it, and ship it off. All those mysteries I'd been devouring offered me a glimpse of the potential order I could bring to my own story, a way to rewrite my life. Based on the number of people who line up after my writing workshops for a private word, or who contact me online, I know I'm not alone. There are many of us who need to reprocess our garbage, but who can't bear the idea of writing memoir, whether it's because we are too close to the trauma, don't want to hurt or be hurt by those we're writing about, or simply prefer the vehicle of fiction.

I kept up writing *May Day*, rubbing it like a worrystone, afraid to relapse into that gaping darkness where I was the monster. I wrote about laughter, the unexpected, a woman startled by the death of someone she loves. She thinks she's responsible but is held up by unexpected allies. In the end, she solves the mystery of his death.

May Day is an uneven book, my first real novel.

It's entirely fictional and was deeply therapeutic to write.

When I typed the last word of that book, I knew the darkness would never return, not at the level that I'd experienced that day with Zoë, not in a way that had the power to obliterate me.

The research would tell you that I was externalizing the story, habituating myself to it, inoculating myself against deep grief by exposing myself to it in small, controlled doses. All I knew was that my brain wasn't spinning as much and I was beginning to feel again, even if it was the emotions of fictional characters. Little by little, I was carving out new space for thoughts that were not about death or depression. Through the gentle but challenging exercise of writing a novel, I was learning how to control stories, which is what our lives are—stories.

I'm not the first writer to discover this healing process.

Charles Dickens' *David Copperfield* is his public grappling with some of his more haunting childhood experiences, including a complicated, troubled relationship with his father. In addition to Dickens declaring *David Copperfield* his most autobiographical and favorite of all the novels he wrote, *The Guardian* places it at number fifteen in a list of the one hundred best novels in history.

Tim O'Brien is a Vietnam War veteran whose *The Things They Carried* is about a Vietnam War veteran named Tim O'Brien. The work is fiction. He coalesces something fundamental, something almost mystical at the heart of rewriting your life, when he writes in his most famous book, "A thing may happen and be a total lie; another thing may not happen and be truer than the truth." *The Things They Carried* has sold over two million copies internationally, won numerous awards, and is an English classroom staple.

Isabel Allende was the first writer to hold me inside a sentence, rapt and wondrous. It's no surprise that her most transformative writing springs from personal anguish. Her first book, *The House of the Spirits*, began as a letter to her dying grandfather whom she could not reach in time. *Eva Luna*, one of my favorite novels, is about an orphan girl who uses her storytelling gift to survive and thrive amid trauma, and Allende refers to the healing power of writing in many of her interviews. Allende's books have sold over fifty-six million copies, been translated into thirty languages, and been made into successful plays and movies. Such is the power of mining your deep.

Jeanette Winterson acknowledges that her novel *Oranges Are Not the Only Fruit* is her own story of growing up gay in a fundamentalist Christian household in the 1950s. She wrote it to create psychic space from the trauma. In her memoir, she writes of *Oranges*, "I wrote a story I could live with. The other one was too painful. I could not survive it."

Sherman Alexie, who grew up in poverty on an Indian reservation that as a child he never dreamed he could leave, does something similar in his young adult novel, *The Absolutely True Diary of a Part-time Indian*, named one of the "Best Books of 2007" by *School Library Journal*. He has said that fictionalizing life is so satisfying because he can spin the story better than real life did.

Nora Ephron's roman à clef *Heartburn* is a sharply funny, fictionalized account of Ephron's own marriage to Carl Bernstein. She couldn't control his cheating during her pregnancy or the subsequent dissolution of their marriage, but through the novelization of her experience, she got to revise the ending of that particular story. In *Heartburn*, Rachel, the character based on Ephron, is asked by a friend why she must make everything a story. Her answer speaks directly to the power of rewriting your life: "Because if I tell the story, I control the version. Because if I tell the story, I can make you laugh, and I would rather have you laugh at me than feel sorry for me. Because if I tell the story, it doesn't hurt as much. Because if I tell the story, I can get on with it." *Heartburn* is Ephron's first published novel. In addition to being a bestseller, her screenplay was turned into a box-office hit starring Meryl Streep and Jack Nicholson.

This alchemy of transmuting-pain-into-gold isn't the purview of an elite group of gifted, well-trained authors who were born with pen in hand. You too can access this power. When I wrote *May Day*, I had an English degree but had never taken a novel-writing class. I didn't even know the basics of writing a short story, let alone had I met a person who actually wrote books. Plus, I was living in rural Minnesota and, pre-Internet (at least where I lived), I had no access to writing groups. I taught myself to write a novel.

Nor is the therapeutic power of novel writing exclusive to those who have experienced deep trauma. Dr. Pennebaker found that directed, expressive writing is beneficial for everyone, meeting us where we are, whether we're coming to terms with a difficult commute, struggling against an annoying coworker, navigating a divorce, or coping with deep grief or PTSD.

You don't even have to want to publish what you write, and in fact, it's okay if you don't. Undertake this journey as if your writing is for your eyes only. You can always change your mind about publishing, but if you begin from the perspective that your writing is private, you give yourself permission to write freely and with integrity without polluting your story with the fickle demands of the publishing world, because here's the truth: it doesn't matter if you burn the novel the second you finish penning it. You can even toss it in the air, still burning, fire bullets into it, pour acid on it when it falls, and bury the ashes. You'll *still* reap all the physical and psychological benefits of writing it. The balm and insight lie in externalizing and controlling the story, not in showing it to others.

If and when you do decide to publish, though, you'll have something genuine and powerful to offer the world. Dickens, Alexie, O'Brien, Ephron, Allende, Winterson, and hundreds of other bestselling authors created compelling stories because they pulled them from a place of truth, vulnerability, and experience. Turning crucible moments into a novel is not only regenerative for the writer, but it's also glorious for the reader. That authenticity creates an indelible story.

So, now you know what brought me here. It wasn't Jay's suicide that was my rock bottom. It was what I let grief do to me, how I allowed it to sneak up and turn me against my child. You also know how I dug myself out—writing fiction. I didn't know the science behind narrative therapy, though it was already firmly established. I just sensed that I *had* to write, and it had to be fiction.

I am staking out this territory.

I'm calling it *rewriting your life*.

I'm inviting you to visit. Stay as long as you want. Redecorate, even.

This book is your map to this land. It puts the merciful, transformative, and very possibly profitable power of novel writing in your hands. It combines the science of narrative and expressive therapy with the practice of novel writing and a juicy vein of "I'll show you mine, so you can show you yours." The result, I hope, will be your prescription for health and renewal from wherever you are, something you can accomplish any place, anytime, cheaply, alone or with others. Above all, this journey will be gentle and humane, and the end result will be a novel with the bones to be great.

You don't have to believe any of this.

You just have to do it.

This is the power of writing.

CHAPTER 2

KNOW THYSELF

If you do not tell the truth about yourself you cannot tell it about other people.

—Virginia Woolf

We move what we're learning from our heads to our hearts through our hands. We are born makers, and creativity is the ultimate act of integration—it is how we fold our experiences into our being.

—Brené Brown

In *Opening Up: The Healing Power of Expressing Emotions*, expressive therapy pioneer Dr. James W. Pennebaker devotes several chapters to the history and power of personal honesty. According to his extensive studies, all humans have inappropriate thoughts, fears, and uncomfortable memories. The best way to move past them is to travel through them.

In other words, the truth will set you free.

Perhaps like me, you find this vastly comforting.

Building off social psychologist Dr. Dan Wegner's findings that the harder we try to bury a thought, the more power it gains (the "try not to think of a white bear" hypothesis), Pennebaker designed studies that found that when you stop suppressing and instead reveal your negative thoughts and memories, even if only on paper, you create a narrative congruence that allows your brain to release them.

Although Pennebaker's studies cannot pinpoint whether the relief comes from the act of releasing a secret or the cessation of the work of inhibiting it, the science is clear: disclosing your closet skeletons is good for your immune system, your mental health, your blood pressure, your heart rate, and a bunch of your other parts. In an elegant and interesting twist to his work, Pennebaker discovered in one particular study that the "sickest" subjects (as measured by the frequency of doctor visits) were also the people who wrote on the most superficial topics when asked to write nonstop on any subject for ten minutes, "whereas the healthy students' writing samples were broader in scope, more emotional, and more self-reflective" (61). The least healthy students wrote about the weather and their clothes, while the fittest explored relationships and the meaning of life. They were willing to make themselves vulnerable on the page.

Going deep makes us healthy, and healthy people go deep.

WHY GOOD WRITERS ARE SELF-AWARE

If deep self-awareness is crucial to mental and physical health, it's also the key to the candy store when it comes to crafting powerful fiction. According to author Joanne Harris' Writer's Manifesto, writers' most important task is to be true to themselves. Natalie Goldberg, in her awesome *Writing Down the Bones*, calls this state of authenticity "metaphor":

> *It comes from a place that is very courageous, willing to step out of our preconceived ways of seeing things and open so large that it can see the oneness in an ant and in an elephant. . . Your mind is leaping, your writing will leap, but it won't be artificial. (37)*

Jeff Davis, author of *The Journey from the Center to the Page: Yoga Philosophies and Practices as Muse for Authentic Writing*, offers further insight on the necessity of writing authentically: "Part of writing the truth includes exploring the truth of our self (or selves)" (193). He doesn't mean writing memoir; he means writing honestly. According to Davis, a straightforward retelling of an event lacks the depth and complexity needed to create a powerful narrative. As writers, we must make connections by exploring the choices that led us to one outcome or another as well as the forces beyond our control, all of which leads naturally to an exploration of this mortal coil.

Deepening our self-exploration naturally results in deeper storylines in our fiction and in complex characters that speak to the universal human experience. Foregrounding these collective truths means readers will see themselves in your tale, but only if you tell it true. I've seen this proven time and again in my two decades of teaching creative writing, where I've discovered one constant: people who live unexamined lives write boring stories. If you don't know the truth about yourself, you are not equipped to touch on bigger truths, and writing without a profound level of personal and thus universal honesty is nothing more than a fancy grocery list.

Renowned writers agree. Eudora Welty claimed that the novel is the most truthful of all artistic mediums. According to Stephen King, compelling fiction is the truth inside the lie. Tennessee Williams describes writers as the opposite of magicians: magicians create an illusion that looks like truth, but a novelist hides the truth behind the impression of fiction. Barbara Kingsolver argues that a writer's main job is to figure out what she has to say that no one else can. Kurt Vonnegut, with his usual humor, said, "Do you realize that all great literature is all about what a bummer it is to be a human being? Isn't it such a relief to have somebody say that?"

To discover your unique message, you must know yourself.

It's not just writers who recognize this; readers understand it as well. Think of the last book that captured you and pulled you inside its sweet pages. What do you remember about it? What resonated with you? I'm willing to bet it wasn't "The main character did this and this and then that." Compelling fiction offers more than a list of events. It offers Truth about ourselves and the world we live in.

Do you see where I'm going with this? Fiction is, paradoxically, the most honest mode of expression, and you can't write it if you don't practice it in your own life, any more than someone who doesn't swim can be a lifeguard. You have to be true to your roots. It is where you find your voice, what *you* need to write about, what you have the juice to make worth reading. You must first know yourself to write authentic fiction, the kind of fiction that transforms and heals you.

CULTIVATING DEEPER SELF-AWARENESS

Like every other part of the learning-to-rewrite-your-life process, I stumbled upon the importance of this know-yourself-before-you-write purely by accident. At the time, I was searching for a different kind of truth: the reason Jay had chosen suicide. I contacted his ex-fiancée, credit card company, doctor, realtor, coworkers, brother, and went through every scrap of paper he had in storage to dig up answers. It became a full-time job, an obsession. Three months later, when I was beginning to wonder if the truth I was chasing was undiscoverable, I adopted a puppy. Four months in and still no answers in sight, I found myself impractically daydreaming about famous actors coming to save me from my grief. It was usually Matt Damon because he's cute and seems handy but also sometimes Kevin Bacon because I'm a child of the '80s and have eyes. There was even a period when I waited for the first Steve from *Blue's Clues* to come and rescue me.

This tells you how destroyed I was. It also tells you an uncomfortable much about how I spent my downtime.

When my search for an outer truth dead-ended, I aimed it inward. I had a predisposition to head this direction as I've always been Manson-girl intense about personal accountability, of which self-awareness is a crucial piece. The scariest movies to me were always the ones in which a creature took ownership of another's will. *The Blob. Invasion of the Body Snatchers.* The first *Spy Kids*, because in it, secret agents were turned into incoherent thumb creatures. I lose sleep over being blind to my own faults. Like Christopher McCandless' parents. Did you read *Into the Wild*? That man and woman destroyed their son, and by all accounts, to this day they choose to believe he was simply a free spirit following the wind. There is nothing more horrible to me than accidentally hurting others. It made sense, then, that in the wake of Jay's suicide, I turned over every stone in myself to discover if maybe the *why* was hidden there.

My wonderful therapist at the time recommended journaling as a way to organize this rigorous self-examination. I demurred for two reasons: (1) At that point in my life, I'd never really journaled and it seemed like a lot of treading word-water, and (2) I'm chickenshit. In fact, that's what I initially called writing behind the veil of fiction: chickenshitography. I still like the name, but the truth you will soon discover (as I did) is that it doesn't really describe the process.

Knowing yourself is no task for a coward.

Writing *May Day* took the place of journaling for me. I pumped my fears, my insecurities, my need for justice and answers into that novel. The fact that I became self-aware *during* the writing of it is one of the reasons it's such an uneven book, and also why I recommend you undertake this chapter's writing exercise before you dig into your novel. You'll save yourself time if your compass is pointed true in advance.

Healing yourself, healing others, and creating powerful fiction are not the only reasons to confess to yourself. You'll also discover soon enough—if you don't know it already—that writing novels serves as both a shield and a microscope. That's why it's important to reach a certain level of self-awareness in advance. You don't want to accidentally share an embarrassing secret you meant to conceal or dig deep into a memory you aren't ready to explore. Eventually, of course, you'll examine it all. That's the beauty of writing fiction. You'll peek in your own dark cracks, and it'll feel like playing. But you need a scan of your own internal terrain so you can control the process.

In shorthand: know thyself.

Take the whole of who you are and put it on paper, first in a journal in its undistilled form and then in your novels in its fictionalized shape. Because you know what? All our ugliness, fears, joys, and journeys are more similar than they are different, and when you're honest with yourself, you can be honest with your writing, and when you're honest with your writing, it reverberates. It connects. It makes people say, "I'm not the only one."

Let me demonstrate by telling you a story.

Several winters back, I was returning from Tae Kwon Do with my kids. We'd moved from the rural house where Jay spoke his last words to a 1940s bungalow in a conservative central Minnesota city. My kids were six and ten.

We used to hit Tae Kwon Do every Tuesday and Thursday, and every Tuesday and Thursday, we returned to our little house in St. Cloud at 8:30 p.m. It was always the same routine except for one Thursday in early March. When we returned home that night, there was a potted begonia resting on our back step. The temperature was hovering around twelve degrees above zero, but that begonia was green-leaved and fresh in its brown paper bag, its tender orange petals silky.

Somebody knew exactly when we were returning home and had timed their flower-leaving accordingly. Five more minutes, and it would have been frozen solid.

My kids thought it was a nice gesture, and I encouraged that. In my head, though, I was thinking: *We've recently moved to town. We don't know anyone here. All my friends and family live at least thirty minutes away. No one who drove that far would leave a flower on my back step without a note. Clearly, a serial killer has been tracking me and my babies for weeks, has learned when we come and go, and he's leaving his calling card—the orange begonia—right before he murders us in our sleep.*

That night, I slept on the couch nearest the front door holding a knife. It was my chef's knife without the tip, which I had broken off a couple years earlier in a pound of frozen ground turkey that wasn't thawing fast enough. It was the sharpest blade I had, but that's hardly the point, is it?

SOMEBODY LEFT ME A FLOWER, AND IT MADE ME SLEEP WITH A KNIFE.

It wasn't just that once. There's something about having kids that super-revs the power of catastrophic thinking. At that time, I was traveling to conferences and out-of-state signings about a dozen times a year, and I left my kids with my parents. Every time I went, I said the same thing to my mom: "Don't forget you're watching them."

And she always said the same thing back. "Don't worry. I raised you, remember?"

I might not be her best reference.

I remember how many times she let me walk to the store alone when I was five, or how she encouraged me to miss two weeks of fifth grade because we didn't like the politics of the long-term sub. But I get her point. I survived, and my kids would, too.

Still, when my plane left the ground or my wheels crossed the state line, my catastrophic thinking kicked in. What if my babies were kidnapped? Would I be able to find them? Could I go on living if I didn't? Or if they ended up in the hospital, how long would it take me to get back to them? What do you even think about when you're waiting to get a flight back to your children in a hospital? Should I call and make sure they're okay? Or should I wait until I've been gone five minutes?

Agh.

And don't even get me started on public speaking. You know how people say, "It was an honor just to be nominated?" I mean it. I like staying in the audience. I worry every time I speak in front of a crowd of people I respect that I'll start bleating like a sheep right before my bowels relax.

So there you have it. The true confessions of a catastrophic thinker. I imagine there is a medication for it, but I am certain that the same part of my brain that takes these wicked spirals is the part that allows me to love reading and spinning stories. All it takes is a spark, and I can run with it. (The superstitious part of me is also sure that thinking about all this stuff is protection *against* it happening. Sorry, author of the *The Secret*.)

This is My Own Special Blend of crazy™. I know exactly where it lives in my brain, and that's where I go to harvest the humor when I need it in my writing. That connection with my weirdness keeps my work authentic. You have your own unique foibles, and you should be honest about them. You should also mine the mother-loving daylights out of them because that intersection of vulnerability and creativity is where your voice and your fire live.

Don't just *assume* you know yourself, by the way. We all don our masks, and we do it so often that often we wear them home. In fact, despite my lifetime of worrying and seeking personal authenticity, it was my *incredibly* uncomfortable Kickstarter campaign in 2014—a request for help in funding the self-publishing of my magical realism novel—that made me realize how much I censor myself in my daily life. I'm not talking about being unkind or insensitive to others. I don't condone either. I'm talking about overthinking everything I say or write for fear of accidentally offending someone, of shaving off my edges so no one is ruffled, of being bland and funny and helpful. None of that serves me, or the people I love, or most importantly to this moment, my writing.

To write well, you must know and be yourself, at least on the page.

TRUTH BEFORE TALE

I've created a simple, three-part journaling exercise to help you increase your self-awareness as well as nudge you toward thinking about how to apply it in your writing. It's called Truth Before Tale. You can find it in its entirety at the end of the chapter, but here's an overview:

Step One Crack open that notebook you straightaway got your hands on after reading this book's introduction. Starting on the first page, freewrite on five topics for ten minutes per topic. If you're unfamiliar, freewriting means writing without judgment, fear, or correction. It's about quantity rather than quality. Turning off your inner critic is crucial to the writing process, and giving yourself permission to freewrite is the quickest way to achieve that. The five topics you will freewrite on: what you are most scared of, what you are proudest of, what your greatest strengths are, your deepest shame, and most importantly, what you're most seeking in life.

Step Two Carry the notebook around for three days and write down your mental chatter three times each of those three days. I recommend setting a timer to remind yourself to do this. This step provides insight into what your mind is up to when you're not paying attention.

Step Three Cull the information you uncovered in Step One and Step Two, neat and sweet, gathering what resonates and leaving the rest. Begin to consider how you can use this material in your novel. It's okay if you don't have an idea for your novel yet. Just go with the process.

In the hopes that it is helpful to you, I'm going to show you my Step Three below. No way would I ever show you my Step One and Step Two, though. They are messy and incoherent and terrifying. I expect yours will be, as well, and that it might be hard to let the truth spill out on paper. Remember that you don't need to show it to anyone. If that assurance isn't enough, I recommend you plan on ripping out the pages and burning them when you're done writing them. I'm serious. You need to access the past and the truth, but you shouldn't live there. Getting it out will provide relief, and you'll have enough to create Step Three from memory, which is the only step you need for writing your novel.

My Step Three below is the result of freewriting on each of the five topics in Step One (scared of, proud of, strengths, shame, life goals) and randomly checking in with my brain à la Step Two. Finally, when organizing the information from those two steps, I started to think about how I could use it in my writing. Here goes. Please, think about your own Step Three while you read mine.

What I'm Most Scared Of

Turns out my biggest fear is being myself, my whole, lovely-ugly Jessie, and having people laugh and point. Here are the parts of me that I shave off so as to be bland and easily inserted into a variety of social situations, as well as to not turn off potential readers:

I'm a little bit raunchy. I like to swear. Fuck. See? I liked typing that. Fuckity fuck.

I'm regularly inappropriate. For example, the other day, my son asked if he could buy Axe body spray. I said, "No, because it'll shrink your testicles." He was twelve at the time. He was horrified, but he didn't question me. I call that good parenting (that stuff smells like the thigh juice of musk oxen crammed on a sun-cooked bus packed with Mediterranean playboys), but it might make others squeamish. So I didn't post it on Facebook, but I've been dying to share it with someone. That someone is you.

I'm a liberal. And a feminist. I shy away from sharing anything political because I'm a Minnesotan, I don't want to silence people or give the impression I know everything, and I don't want people to be mean to me or reject me, but I'm about as liberal as they come. I support civil rights including gay marriage, I like clean air and healthy food, I believe in investing in people rather than corporations, and I think every mentally healthy person wants to be a productive member of society and take care of themselves and their family and so should get *at least* as many opportunities as I have to live where they want to live, take out a loan, be considered for a job on their merits rather than gender or race or sexuality, and have access to quality education. All that good stuff. I also enjoy informed disagreement (my friends and family do not all share my opinions) and am fine with the "I don't knows." Willful ignorance, though? Makes me rage.

My sense of humor is not always kosher. I sometimes think weird things are funny. Weird, horrible things like that Internet photo of two action figure GI Joes perched on the corpse of a roadkill squirrel as if they've just hunted it on safari.

Some days, I'm crabby, uninspired, and scared. Scared that people will hate my writing, worried that people will see right through me and turn away, afraid that whatever spark it is that keeps me wanting to tell stories and write books will disappear and I'll feel lost. This means that I'm not always funny or interesting. My funny is a dial-up superpower rather than a Wi-Fi one.

I am not religious, but I am spiritual. I'm pretty far from having this one figured out, but what it means in practice is that I will treat other people as I would like to be treated, and I might sometimes talk about meditating or gratitude or positive visualization and looking for (and seeing) magic on a regular basis—my daughter's gorgeous smile, the light shining through lemon-colored fall leaves, my son choosing being kind over being right, dreaming about someone from high school one night and seeing the person for the first time in ten years the next day, that sort of thing.

My biggest fear is letting all the "real me" listed above out into the world and being resoundingly rejected. How to use it in service of my writing? I channel my inappropriate humor and love of swearing into Mrs. Berns, the oversexed octogenarian who is my favorite character in my first mystery series. The fear of being vilified for my far-left politics and of letting people down for not always being "on" manifests as the protagonist's fish-out-of-water, city-girl-in-a-small town conflict that runs throughout those same books. Once I claimed my spirituality and my belief in what I call kitchen magic, I realized I wanted more of it in my life and wrote the magical realism book whose self-publishing I funded through my Kickstarter campaign. I sense there is more to excavate there, so I plan to expand that book into a series.

What I Am Most Proud Of

It's interesting to me that of the six terrifying writing prompts required of the Truth Before Tale Exercise, this one was the hardest for me. Claiming my achievements, once I forced myself to dig deeper than the culturally encouraged "my kids are my greatest accomplishment," was hard. But outside of them, I am most proud of my writing. In fact, I think I'm a good writer and sometimes, a great one. My first few published books are spotty, but I keep reading and working and listening, and I'm getting better with each novel. I am really, really proud of that, and I'm going to stop apologizing for *May Day*'s rickety plotting, or the fact that I love to write funny, semi-romantic mysteries (among other stuff).

When it comes to using this awareness in service of my writing, I'm interested in exploring how this invisible barrier between me and claiming my achievements operates. Do other people experience this? Can I use it to create a character with an internal conflict exactly like this, a character who appears strong and confident but secretly refuses to own her accomplishments? Why would she do that? I actually made a note in my notebook to come back to this because I think it'll provide interesting complexity to a private investigator character I'm currently creating.

My Greatest Strengths

Curiosity, belief in constant self-evolution that looks more like running down a steep hill and trying not to fall than an organized plan, and a short memory for wrongs done to me. These are my strengths. That last one always surprises me because if you met me, you'd understandably peg me as a grudge-holder. I like to control situations, I'm assertive, and my humor can be sharp. But damn if I can remember bad things with any clarity. My temper burns hot and quick, and I move on. I like that about me, and the other two qualities, too. And at least one of these three makes it into every main character, or protagonist, that I write because that allows me to write them authentically. I can feel the pleasure of having these strengths, and if I can feel it, I can write it so much better. This is important because your protagonists must be flawed, and so you need the strengths to balance them out.

My Deepest Shame

My deepest shame is running out on Zoë. In the spirit of demonstrating this whole exercise for you, however, I'll share my second deepest shame, and you'll wonder how that kid ever survived childhood.

When I held newborn Zoë, I experienced true love for the first time. So as not to paint you too rosy a picture, this was after twenty-eight hours of labor toward the end of which I screamed, "I don't care if you *bring the janitor in here*, if he can get this kid out of me." Still, my immediate love for her was the most honest, most powerfully clean emotion I'd ever felt. That amazing, gorgeous kid turned my world inside out and upside down in the best possible way. That's why I was so deeply ashamed that, for the first year of her life, I could not hold a knife while she was in the same room with me. I was consumed by a powerful, irrational fear that somehow, the knife would slip from my hand, fly through the air, and puncture her soft spot.

POP.

Seriously. At the time, this scenario seemed as real as my own hands.

I did everything I could to chase that visual out of my head, but I couldn't (*don't think about a white bear don't think about a white bear*). It was horrifying and shameful. How could my thoughts be so violent and dark toward something so innocent?

I thought I was the worst mom in the world, and I certainly didn't tell anyone. I'd just tuck Zoë in that little swing chair safely in the other room while I cooked. She'd have to be on the other side of a wall, out of sight, because if I could see her that meant the knife could reach her. Fighting off the mental image of the blade flying out of my hands as I sliced was so painful that I often wept as I cooked.

After Z's first birthday, right around the same time I stopped breastfeeding, that weird obsession with the knife disappeared. *Poof.* One day it was there, overwhelming me, and the next day it was gone. I'd never experienced anything like it before, and thankfully, it didn't return with the birth of my son. In fact, I forgot completely about it until a couple years later when my aunt dropped in casual conversation that her friend, after the birth of her first child, became consumed by a terror that she'd somehow put the baby in the chest freezer and forget she was there. This new mother was also a pediatrician, was mentally healthy, and had never before experienced that kind of thought. Of course, she'd never forget her baby in the chest freezer, but she couldn't stop imagining that she would.

Apparently, postpartum intrusive thoughts, this sort of "I so badly don't want to hurt my baby that all I can think about is hurting my baby," are common. If I had told someone about it, or at least written it down, I could have released it and saved myself a year of torment. It emerged when freewriting for Step One, though, and I will definitely include that character trait in a future protagonist because it is real and true and will subsequently give that character a resonance with the millions of other women who have experienced postpartum intrusive thoughts. In fact, the battle against these thoughts would make a powerful subplot to any book.

What I'm Most Seeking in Life

Ah. This one is the money shot. This is where you'll harvest the plot for your novel because what *you* are after is what at least one of your *characters* will be after. The famous axiom "write what you know" isn't only about making a character a teacher because you're a teacher or setting a story in Chicago because you know your way around Navy Pier. It's about exploring your emotional terrain through a fictional character. My life goals are true love, healthy kids, self-esteem, justice, money. You better believe that's what any character I'm going to follow around for a year wants also.

Everything you just read is my Step Three list, the one I tend like a garden—planting, watering, weeding—so I can harvest it to write authentic characters.

What's your list look like?

This is important. It's your foundation as a writer.

As you complete the Truth Before Tale, remember that your truths are not constant.

They are not your epitaph.

They *are*, however, what are going to get you through this next year. Best-selling and laugh-out-loud-funny writer Anne Lamott calls your authentic memories your raw clay, the thing from which you mold your story and the people in it. I call it your ink and your heartbeat for the next year. You're going to need both, so put them where you can see them while you write your book.

Trust me.

Oh and hey, that orange begonia? Turns out it had been left on my doorstep by an old college friend who'd heard I'd moved back to town. She dropped it off on a whim and hadn't left a note because she didn't have a pen. See? All my worrying scared off the serial killer.

TRUTH BEFORE TALE

Step One, Day One

Freewrite.

1. Carve out fifty minutes in your schedule.

2. Crack open your notebook.

3. Write each of these prompts on five different pages, one prompt per page, leaving a blank page as a cushion between each.

   a. I am most scared of . . .

   b. I am most proud of . . .

   c. My greatest strengths are . . .

   d. My deepest shame is . . .

   e. What I'm most seeking in life is . . .

4. Set your timer for ten minutes. Freewrite on the first prompt. When the timer goes off, reset it for another ten minutes and freewrite on the second prompt, and so on, until you've written for ten minutes on each of the five prompts. When it comes to freewriting, there is only one rule: quantity, not quality. The point is to write down whatever comes into your head without criticism, without worrying about grammar, without stopping, until the timer goes off. Freewriting is the shortest cut to your wisdom. Dive in, do it unabashedly, and remember that you can burn what you write after you're done. You'll still get all the value from this mile marker.

Step Two, Days Two to Four

Surprise-Visit Your Brain

Carry the notebook with you for three days. Schedule a reminder to go off three separate times each of those days, making sure to set it for times when you'll be able to write, uninterrupted, for five minutes at a time. When the timer goes off, write down what you were thinking about. The more honest you are about this self-chatter, the better. Prepare to be either horrified or bored at what you spend time thinking about. Or both. Borrified.

Step Three, Day Five

Organize

Reread your five freewriting entries (or mentally revisit them if you burned them) and your nine surprise visit entries. Underline what stands out to you, using it to create a personal sketch as I've done on the previous pages. It's for your eyes only. Be candid.

At the end of each sketch, write at least two sentences speculating how you could use what you've discovered as either a character trait or a plotline in your novel, similar to what I've done in my Step Three example. Don't worry if you're vague at this point. Each exercise in this book builds on the one before it, so you'll be guided toward how to develop your novel at each step in the process.

PART II

THE TOOLS OF
YOUR
TRANSFORMATION

CHAPTER 3

READ LIKE A WRITER

We read books to find out who we are. What other people, real or imaginary, do and think and feel . . . is an essential guide to our understanding of what we ourselves are and may become.

—Ursula K. Le Guin

The more that you read, the more things you will know. The more that you learn, the more places you'll go.

—Dr. Seuss

Reading is the finest teacher of how to write.

—Annie Proulx

When my kids were young—Zoë, five; Xander, two—I made up a bedtime story called *Claude the Dragon*. Claude was a benevolent, iridescent beast that flew around the world with Princess Zoë and Prince Xander[1] saddled to his back. Through lively adventures, the royal kids learned the importance of sharing, picking up after themselves, and not calling people "stinky pooplickers," no matter how high the stakes.

---

[1]   I swear that when I told my kids that the prince and princess in this story had the same names as them, Zoë looked at me, eyes wide, and muttered, "What are the odds?"

Up until Claude entered our lives, I'd been reading the kids three picture books every night before bedtime. Three seemed like the perfect amount. Not so few that they'd snitch to strangers that I was a bad mom but not so many that I'd fall face-to-*It's Pajama Time!* after a sixteen-hour day of teaching/raising kids/writing/worrying that I wasn't good enough.

Making up a bedtime story after the three-books-a-night routine grew stale seemed surprisingly sane, in a Ma Ingalls "Don't be ridiculous, of course, I'll sew your clothes and make your pancakes from scratch after I tap that tree outside for the maple syrup so you know I love you, what other options are there?" sort of way. Plus, I was an author, or at least that's what I was telling myself. This was back in 2003. I'd written my first mystery, was searching for an agent, and I'd begun to draft the second in the series. If I could write a whole novel for strangers, I could make up a bedtime story for my kids, for Pete's sake. That way, when they were themselves famous and wrote their own memoirs, they'd have only positive things to say about me, right?[2]

This was how *Claude the Dragon* was born.

I should tell you that I am not an oral storyteller. It's a ridiculously rare and important gift, and so if you know someone who makes you lean forward in your seat because you are hanging off their last word to find out how the story ends, hug them for me. You are a lucky duck. Not so much Zoë and Xander. They got your garden variety, "Claude the Dragon is shiny and scaled and brave. He picks up Princess Zoë and Prince Xander and takes them places to do important things."

Z and X were good sports about being "read" these Claude adventures. After all, they were the centers of the stories, there was a dragon, and Mommy wasn't crying from exhaustion.

Good, good, and good.

But when they grew old enough to read on their own, Zoë three years later with Harry Potter and Xander five years after that thanks to Captain Underpants, I was happy to drop Claude. He never visited again.

---

2   This is an actual question.

So spend a little time with the surprise I felt when, just last week, now-seventeen-year-old Zoë brought him up. It was her favorite story. She loved Claude, she said. She still sometimes thinks about him, just like she would think about a friend she misses.

That ability to connect is the magic in stories.

If you were fortunate enough to be read to when you were young, you know this instinctively. Claude the Dragon taught my kids that they mattered and that they were safe in this world. Think back to your own favorite childhood book. Can you see the cover? Does it create a physical reaction? For me, the first book I loved was *The Monster at the End of This Book, Starring Lovable, Furry Old Grover*. Part of it was that I do a passable Grover imitation and there wasn't a lot of call for that in other areas of my life. A bigger reason was that the book spoke to me. It inspired me not to be afraid of what was around the corner. Rereading it as an adult, it also reminds me that I'm my own worst monster. That is the power of stories, to work on our psyche, to serve as anchors and guideposts in our lives.

So, what did your favorite childhood book teach you?

Maybe more importantly, what can you learn from the fiction that you read now?

Lots, it turns out.

While it's obvious what you learn from reading nonfiction—a book on raising your children teaches you how to introduce new vegetables to their diet, a book on decorating your kitchen tells you how to reface cupboards—you might not know that researchers have found tangible benefits to reading fiction as well. Immersing yourself in a good novel increases your understanding of self and others. Studies suggest this is due to something called embodied cognition, in which your brain thinks your body is doing something it isn't. Athletes use embodied cognition when they visualize making a shot, thereby preparing them to do exactly that when it matters. Specific to reading fiction, your brain drops you into the body of the protagonist, experiencing what they experience, which expands your capacity to put yourself in another's shoes. In addition to increasing empathy, neurobiological research proves that reading fiction changes the biology of the brain, making it more receptive and connected. Reading novels also makes you more creative and open-minded, gives you psychological courage, and keeps your brain active and healthy.

The therapeutic value of reading novels is so profound that it has birthed something called bibliotherapy, in which clients are matched with a literary fiction designed to address what is ailing them, from mild depression to a troubled intimate relationship to a desire to find a work/family balance. Anyone who belongs to a book club has likely experienced a version of fiction's healing powers.

The value of reading is even more significant if you're a writer. Imagine being a chef who eats only chicken nuggets, a carpenter who refuses to look at buildings, or an orchestra conductor who doesn't listen to anything but commercial jingles. Such is the problem for a writer who doesn't read regularly and widely.

Books are the maps to your craft.

According to Stephen King, "If you don't have the time to read, you don't have the time (or the tools) to write. Simple as that."

I agree.

HOW TO READ LIKE A WRITER

Learning to read like a writer is a practice in self-awareness and critical analysis. You need to be mindful when you really like a book/movie/song, or, even more telling, when you are actively turned off by one. Reading like a writer requires you to get in touch with that self-awareness and hone it by asking questions. I'm going to call that piece your narrative detective—its job is to solve the mystery of the narrative, looking at the ways it is and isn't succeeding—and I'm going to encourage you to feed it PIE every time you read *anything*: a menu, a short story, the interpretive plaque next to the world's biggest redwood tree. A book.

Here are the ingredients to the PIE:

- **Prepare** with pen and paper. Always have your notebook and something to write with nearby when you read. Your goal is to be prepared for insight. In addition to reading for pleasure, you will now use words as research and write down what you learn. If you prefer, you can dictate into a recorder or type into the Notes section of your phone.

- **Immerse**. Get inside the words, the sentences, the story arc. Don't simply stay on the surface of what you're reading, no matter how shallow it seems. Go deep.

- **Examine**. If that cereal box makes you excited to eat the sugar doodles, ask yourself what it is about the words and their formatting is doing that for you. If you read that redwood plaque and walk away feeling smart, ask yourself how it pierced your busy mind. If—especially if—you're reading a novel, and you connect with a character, or you find yourself yanked out of the story, or you read a sentence twice to savor the citrus taste of it, or anything else of note happens, study that situation like a lover's face. Write down what you think is happening ("main character makes stupid choices," "too many adverbs," "lots of smells make me feel like I'm right there," "each chapter ends with a hook," etc.) because transcribing information flips a switch in our brain, waking up the records guy who then goes over to pick up what you wrote and file it somewhere so you can access it later.

When you feed your narrative detective PIE, she begins to internalize the language and rhythm of story. This level of observation is how most novelists learned to craft their stories. They didn't go to college to learn to be writers. They *read* to learn to be writers. In fact, the first MFA in Creative Writing wasn't offered until 1936, five years after the *New York Times* Bestseller List premiered. Agatha Christie, Mark Twain, and Jane Austen wrote their masterpieces well before that. And most of the current *New York Times* best-selling authors didn't go to college for creative writing. J. K. Rowling's degree is in French. Robert Ludlum studied acting. Ray Bradbury barely graduated high school. The amazing Maya Angelou earned fifty honorary degrees in her lifetime, but she gave birth three weeks after graduating high school and never attended college.

When it came to writing books, all of these writers learned by reading.

You read like a writer to notice how good writing happens so you can emulate it and how bad writing happens so you can avoid it. You learn to understand how a story is strung together, how one particular scene leads to another, to observe how characters are built. I particularly encourage reading in the genre you wish to write in because those stories will have their own unique seasonings. Also, if you have the time and interest, I encourage you to check out Francine Prose's exquisite *Reading Like a Writer: A Guide for People Who Love Books and for Those Who Want to Write Them* for a deeper guided practice on the art of reading like a writer.

It's not only words that you need to pay more attention to on this healing odyssey. You should also start to read *life* like a writer. This is a little bit of a cheat, conflating reading words with reading people, but only a little because when it comes to writing well, inviting your narrative detective to real-life situations and feeding her PIE is just as important as bringing her to written words. You can't take a person you know, whole cloth, and shove them into a story. One, they'll struggle. Two, real people are too big and clumsy for stories. They're inconsistent and often dull if rendered whole. You can—and must— instead take pieces of people, settings, situations and transform them into a story. So walk this world with a pen and notebook in hand, immerse yourself in life, examine why people make the choices they make. Consider what parts work, and which don't, and what you can take away from that to write a compelling novel.

Eavesdrop.

Hang out with people who think differently than you do.

Seek art, particularly art that makes you uncomfortable.

Ask yourself "why" a lot, and then ask yourself "what if." Start answering both questions.

And most importantly, read as if your life depends on it.

CHAPTER 4

PICK YOUR GENRE

Each writer's homework is first to identify his genre, then research its governing practices. And there is no escaping these tasks. We are all genre writers.

—Robert McKee

I do not over-intellectualize the production process. I try to keep it simple: Tell the damned story.

—Tom Clancy

Poetry predates literacy. Western drama appeared in Greece around the fifth century BC. The first novel, however, wasn't published until 1008. It's called *The Tale of Genji*, a tale of court intrigue written by a woman named Murasaki Shikibu. And it wasn't until the eighteenth century that novels became popular, their trajectory tied to the development of the European middle class, growing literacy, and advances in printing.

Back then, novels were considered trashy because they were FUN. If you've got a spare afternoon, I encourage you to Google "scandalous books of the 18th and 19th century" for a giggle. *The Hunchback of Notre Dame* was too saucy for the Catholic Church. Hans Christian Andersen's tales were deemed too violent for Russia. Even back then, novels were shining a light on the themes that make us uncomfortable—sex, violence, fear, the marginalized, what it means to be human.

GENRES

When they first appeared, novels as a whole were considered a genre. Since then, the term has evolved to refer to types of novels: literary (also called mainstream) fiction, romances, Westerns, horror, science fiction, fantasy, mystery, etc. This point is important only if it helps you build the story you want to tell; otherwise, write the book you're writing, and don't give a second thought to genre. I like to know what genre I'm writing in before I begin because it helps me focus the story. It doesn't mean I can't change the genre, or that my publisher won't. It's just easier for me to get somewhere if I know where I'm going. On the other hand, many successful writers simply write the story that's burning inside of them and let their publisher decide how to market it. If you're like me and would feel safer or more organized starting out with a genre, or if it would make your writing feel more productive, then I've got a simple trick to help you choose yours.

Grab your journal and reread it. Your answer to "what do I want most in life" will tell you what genre to write this book in because here's a secret: the governing difference separating one genre from another is what the main character wants the most.

 Remember Chapter 2, "Know Thyself," where you completed the Truth Before Tale? How about Step One of that exercise, where you freewrote on five different prompts? The fifth prompt, the one where you asked what you're most seeking in this life, is the one you need now.

Let me demonstrate below with the eight most popular fiction genres and then go on to give you a little more insight into the defining features of each. Understand that the following is an oversimplification of genres, with a focus on the main character's motivation as the differentiating factor.

- Literary or mainstream fiction: a story in which the protagonist wants to better understand a universal human truth or their place in the world.

- Romance: a story in which the main character wants love.

- Western: a story set in the Old West and in which the main character wants things to be fair, and black and white.

- Horror: a story in which the main character wants to overcome fear and survive.

- Science fiction: a story in which the main character wants to better understand a universal human truth or their place in the world, plus often find an escape, set in the future.

- Fantasy: a story in which the main character needs an object and an adventure (whether they know it or not), set in a fantasy world.

- Mystery (including all its subgenres, such as thrillers and private eye novels): a story in which the main character wants justice.

- Young adult: a story in which the main character is twelve to eighteen years old and wants at least one of the above (the same applies to middle grade, except the main character is eight to twelve years old).

Follow your curiosity like a witching stick to select a genre for the novel you began to write the moment you picked up this book. What story type suits your purpose, gives voice to your pain, worries, and troubles? After Jay's suicide, I burned for answers and justice. I wrote mysteries. Do you crave romance? Write one. Does your tired soul long for a simpler time, when it was clear who were the good guys and who were the bad? Let me introduce you to the Western. Maybe you need a forest fire of fear to rage through your psyche and burn off those branches of terror that keep tripping you. Sounds as though you should write a horror novel, my friend. If you're not sure what you're seeking, you have the perfect recipe for a fantasy in which you can create an object symbolic of your own journey.

Here's more detail on the genres to help you select yours.

Literary Fiction/Mainstream Fiction

Literary, or mainstream, fiction speaks to the human condition and contains threads that reach out beyond the story. Think the *New York Times* best-selling My Struggle series by Karl Ove Knausgaard. On the face of them, these novels are the semi-autobiographical retelling of Knausgaard's life, but he so eloquently and with such fierce honesty touches on the universal human feeling of being misunderstood and out of place that the books transcend the generic coming-of-age tale. Literary/mainstream fiction also foregrounds symbolism, which is where something stands for more than itself, more than the other genres. Theme, an idea that binds the narrative, is a central component. Some popular themes are humans against nature and sacrifice brings reward.

This category of books has no secret superpower (mysteries have suspense, romances have delicious emotion, sci-fi and fantasy have epic world-building, horror has terror, and so on) to carry it through natural story slumps, and so it's got to be solid goodness. The classics, such as novels written by Dickens, Melville, and Wharton, are examples of literary fiction, whereas any book on the *New York Times* Bestseller List that doesn't fit neatly into any other genre is considered general or mainstream fiction. An example of mainstream fiction is Emma Donoghue's *Room*, which she was inspired to write after hearing about the horrific Fritzl case, where Josef Fritzl locked his daughter in the basement for twenty-four years, regularly abusing and raping her, resulting in the birth of seven children. If you've read the book, you're familiar with "Tooth," an incisor used to symbolize the protagonist's connection to his mother. The main theme of this book is the human ability to overcome horrific adversity, and this theme, along with incredible writing and a healthy dose of sideshow curiosity, made this novel a runaway success.

Romance

Romance is the most popular genre, probably because it speaks to the most basic human need: the desire to be loved, to feel a part of something, to belong. Like all the other genres, romance covers a wide spectrum of writing styles, writing levels, and subgenres, including historical romance, romantic suspense, and humorous romance. Think *Gone with the Wind* as an illustration of historical romance. Nora Roberts' *The Obsession,* the love story between a woman abused when she was young and a good-hearted mechanic with the added mystery of an outside obsession running through it, is a great example of romantic suspense, and Jennifer Crusie's *Welcome to Temptation,* described as "blackmail, adultery, murder, vehicular abuse of a corpse, and slightly perverse but excellent sex," as an example of a humorous romance. Regardless of subgenre, a romance is a book based around two people falling in love. While there are barriers to the love, romance novels *must* have a happy ending.

Westerns

The Western genre peaked in the '60s and has been on the decline since, though it's experiencing a resurgence in film, which suggests there's a market for it. The primary element of a Western is its American West setting of the late nineteenth century. Westerns are typically action-packed, often brutal, and feature fast guns and desperate types. Westerns also (usually) explore the lone warrior/pioneer/

cowboy mythos and feature a battered hero or antihero opposite a superbly evil villain. Larry McMurtry's Pulitzer Prize–winning *Lonesome Dove*, the Old West story of an epic cattle drive, is a well-known example of a Western, as is any novel by Louis L'Amour.

Horror

The horror genre has its roots in the Inquisition, which evolved into Gothic novels in the 1700s. Horror novels stand out because of the emotions they evoke: horror, shock, loathing, dread. A good horror novel examines our deepest fears. Popular horror authors include Clive Barker, Stephen King, Angela Carter, and Anne Rice. King's *Cujo*, the story of a rabid St. Bernard that traps a mother and her dying son in a car, and Rice's *Interview with the Vampire*, the wildly popular tale of a modern-day Dracula, epitomize the genre.

Science Fiction/Fantasy

Rod Serling, creator and narrator of the original *The Twilight Zone*, provides the best definition of these two genres that I've ever heard: "Fantasy is the impossible made probable. Science fiction is the improbable made possible." Popularly referred to as the "literature of change," science fiction features an alternate reality that has somehow been affected by science and technology. Typically, scientific principles and concepts are put to work, and the futuristic setting is key. Science fiction asks big questions, as in Margaret Atwood's *The Handmaid's Tale*, which speculates what the future United States will look like if women have no power and are valued only for breeding. Other well-known science fiction authors include Isaac Asimov, Octavia Butler, and Ursula K. LeGuin.

Like science fiction, fantasy is permeated with wonder and set in a magical world. In these other worlds, some sort of magic always figures into the richly imagined story. Often the main character is on a journey, usually seeking an object but sometimes a person. *The Lord of the Rings* is an example, as well as George R. R. Martin's complicated *Game of Thrones* series, where five royal families battle over the throne of Westeros. Marion Zimmer Bradley, Patrick Rothfuss, and Neil Gaiman are also brilliant fantasy writers.

Mystery

Also called crime fiction, mysteries are stories centered on a crime or a puzzle, and the main purpose of the story is to find justice. Mysteries are tightly plotted, with a clear protagonist and antagonist, or "bad guy." A corpse typically appears in the first chapters, clues are provided, subjects are questioned, and red herrings are added until the murder is solved. Popular crime fiction authors include Sir Arthur Conan Doyle, Agatha Christie, Hank Phillippi Ryan, Alison Gaylin, Dan Brown, Catriona McPherson, and Chelsea Cain.

Young Adult

The main distinguishing point of the young adult genre is the age of the protagonist. For young adult, it's twelve to eighteen years old, and for middle grade, it's eight to twelve years old. Young adult fiction is tightly plotted and pulls no punches, is often written using present tense verbs to increase the breakneck pace, and covers raw issues that tweens and teens can identify with. Often adults are subsidiary to the story, and they can also be the antagonists. Examples of young adult literature include *The Hunger Games*, the Harry Potter series, *The Outsiders*, and *The Giver*. While young adult fiction features a protagonist below the age of eighteen, this genre has had explosive appeal to readers of all ages due to its universal themes of disenfranchisement and feeling like an invisible outsider.

Choosing a genre is helpful in guiding your writing process but dangerous to get too hung up on. There's a long history of wildly successful books that don't fit neatly in any genre, despite what their publishers would have you believe: Mary Shelley's *Frankenstein* is both horror and science fiction, Ray Bradbury's *Fahrenheit 451* is literary and science fiction, Stephen King's *11/22/63* is mainstream fiction, Ira Levin's *Rosemary's Baby* is horror and literary fiction, and Audrey Niffenegger's *The Time Traveler's Wife* is both science fiction and romance, to name only a few.

Matthew Clemens, my friend and successful thriller writer, says it best: "There really are only two genres: good books and bad books. Everything else is marketing." Yet, it's helpful at the beginning of a project to *consider* the genre,. In addition, start paying attention to genre as you read if only to make visible the hidden rules of each type, as well as the pros and cons of each specific to your writing goals.

GENRE SELECTION

While selecting a genre is not a necessary step in your novel-writing odyssey, I find it to be a helpful one. If you feel the same way, complete this sentence:

> If I had to select a genre for my novel right now, _____
> makes the most sense because I/my main character wants
> _____ more than anything.

Remember that you are writing a novel, not a contract, and if you want to change your genre later or not select a genre at all, then rock on! This is your book.

CHAPTER 5

CHOOSE YOUR NOVEL CONCEPT

Every secret of a writer's soul, every experience of his life, every quality of his mind, is written large in his works.

—*Virginia Woolf*

Do not hoard what seems good for a later place in the book, or for another book; give it, give it all, give it now.

—*Annie Dillard*

I write to give myself strength. I write to be the characters that I am not. I write to explore all the things I'm afraid of.

—*Joss Whedon*

"There are no bad ideas."

Ever heard that saying?

I know why people utter it. The point is to pop the stopper off the creative faucet, to allow concepts to flow without judgment, to silence the inner critic and create a safe space for brainstorming. Where would we be, after all, if a 6′6″ British writer had decided it'd be stupid to write about a lonely orphan's escape from his evil aunts and subsequent world adventures inside an enormous stone fruit? We'd be without Roald Dahl's *James and the Giant Peach*, a beloved adventure tale inspired by Dahl's premature loss of his father and ill-treatment in British boarding schools. Or, what if Stephen King hadn't scribbled on a cocktail napkin his bizarre dream about a writer captured by a psychotic fan and then gone on to imbue that fan with all the qualities of the drug addiction he was battling? There'd be no *Misery* for us.

So, is it true that when it comes to writing a novel, there are no bad ideas?

Nope. There are *terrible* ideas. Or at least, there are terrible ideas for *you*. And me.

Let me illustrate.

A BAD IDEA

The year is 2006. My first novel has just been published, and I'm on a whirlwind signing tour. Ha ha! Kidding. I was allowed into a handful of Minnesota bookstores where they invariably put me at a table wedged between the bathroom and a display of Ted Nugent's paperback *Kill It and Grill It*. In any case, I am on book tour, and the movie *Eragon* is in theaters. Christopher Paolini started writing the book the film was based on when he was fifteen, and, subsequently, boys all over the nation are inspired to write novels of their own in the hopes that their magnum opus, too, will be turned into a movie. Teenaged boys exactly like the one standing on the other side of my signing table, tucked inside the bowels of a Barnes & Noble.

He's sixteen, tops, and doesn't look like my target audience, but he's at my table, and I'm lonely back by the bathroom, so I slap on a smile and ask him if he likes to read mysteries.

This is what he says by way of response. "I've got an idea for a book."

"Great!" I mean it. I'm starved for conversation. I wouldn't mind talking about his latest algebra assignment. "Tell me about it."

The kid is maybe six foot even and grows taller as he talks. "My idea is for a novel with three central characters, but only one real main character. The one main character, the protagonist, is male, young. He's an orphan who's being raised by his aunt and uncle and has to live under the stairs. He has a mean cousin. They all hate him. What they don't know is that he has magical powers, even though the lightning bolt across his forehead should have given that away."

"Um, what?" I am literally seated across from a display of J. K. Rowling's latest book in a series this kid has just described to me as his own.

"Yeah!" His eyes are on fire now, and he's using his hands to gesture wildly. "The protagonist is a wizard! And his friends break him out of his mean aunt and uncle's house and take him back to the wizard school. It's called Hamworts. Hamworts School of Witchcraft and Wizardry."

I cough politely into my hand. "Is one of his friends male and the other female, and does an old wizard headmaster take them all under his wing back at the wizard school?"

"Yes!"

I try to surreptitiously locate his parent or maybe parole officer. "Hey, that sounds an awful lot like a Harry Potter book," I say gently. Whisper even.

"No!" If anything, he seems even happier. "Everyone in my book is a *hamster*."

I blink like it's my job, unable to speak.

"Totally different," he reassures me.

Totally.

He talked for another ten minutes, telling me about a sorcerer's kibble that Harry Hamster needed to acquire, how he was falling for Hermione Hamster, and how in the end, everything worked out.

I didn't tell him this at the time, but looking back, I think that was a bad idea for a novel.

Not if J. K. Rowling wrote it, of course, and I would love to hear what personal experience she drew on to create a character as multidimensional and compelling as Harry Potter. The sweet kid at my signing, though, had no connection to that outsider-turned-hero story. It meant nothing to him; I don't care how much he loved hamsters. He had no familiarity to call on in writing it, no dream that was driving him—other than the dream of being a billionaire writer—no vision that was his own.

That's why I'm going to amend the saying that there are no bad ideas. For our purposes, the new saying is, "There is no bad idea for a book as long as it has meaning for *you*." Hamsters, wizards, bodacious starfighters, quiet love stories, epic gunfights as the sun cooks the horizon with its blood-orange eye; it's all fair game as long as it is pulled directly from your own personal vault. Your job is to tell *your* stories, not someone else's. It's through this authentic connection that you access your creativity but also that you create compelling fiction.

GOOD IDEAS

Here are three illustrations of best-selling novel ideas with meaning for their writers.

Carrie Fisher
Delusions of Grandma

> Hollywood screenwriter Cora Sharpe learns the meaning of love when she and her mother break her senile grandfather out of a nursing home.

This novel, like most of Fisher's, draws on her experiences as a child of Hollywood and being unlucky in love. You'll certainly recognize the names, like Meryl Streep, that appear in her acknowledgments section, and it doesn't take much sleuthing to recognize fictionalized versions of those people in her writing. Pulling a core theme from her life—the search for love—and playing it out through a fictional plot that relies on composites of friends and family allows Fisher to create an absorbing story that connects with readers.

Ray Bradbury
Dandelion Wine

> Douglas Spaulding explores the joys and fears of being twelve
> years old during a 1928 summer in small-town Illinois.

Bradbury weaves in many of his own adolescent experiences to create
an authentic coming-of-age tale. Green Town, the setting for *Dandelion Wine*, is the fictional name Bradbury gives his hometown of
Waukegan, Illinois. One of the supporting characters, John Huff, is
a real friend of Bradbury's, though Bradbury changed where Huff
lives, some of his characteristics, and creates from whole cloth many
of their interactions, using the genuine feelings he has for Huff as the
foundation upon which he builds the character.

Amy Tan
The Joy Luck Club

> To reconcile her relationship with her immigrant mother,
> American-born Jing-mei Woo must gather her mother's stories
> and travel to China.

Tan explores the theme of what it means to be a mother and a daughter, and specifically the daughter of immigrants, in this and many of
her books. In an interview for *The Joy Luck Club*, Tan says, "When I
was writing, it was so much for my mother and myself . . . I wanted
her to know what I thought about China and what I thought about
growing up in this country." Tan, like her character Jing-mei Woo,
traveled to China for the first time to meet half-siblings. Because
these themes and experiences resonate for Tan, when she fictionalizes
them, they connect with the reader.

You'll notice this pattern across much of successful fiction. Writers explore recurring life themes, using people and experiences from
their own lives upon which to build a cohesive fictional world and
story. But how do you tease out which personal themes are worth

exploring, which relationships are archetypal enough upon which to base a character or conflict, and which scenes or settings from their own life would work in fiction?

RECYCLING YOUR LIFE EXPERIENCES INTO NOVEL IDEAS: A TWO-STEP METHOD

Either what you need to write about is sitting right there on the surface, a big fat emotional wood tick lazily sucking away at your life's blood and that's why you picked up this book, or it's burrowing right under your skin, more of a passive-aggressive bloodsucker, darting out to sabotage a relationship or cobble a life dream before retreating into its scaly sheath to cradle the shredded morsels of your self-esteem.

In either case, you need to pick it off, examine it, and be prepared to dissect it.

Not only will this self-evaluation reveal your novel's central concerns, but it will also give you the tools to repurpose your experiences, a crucial step in turning them into fiction. You see, you cannot simply change the name of the drunk driver who rear-ended your car and put you into the hospital for a week, nor can you move the setting of the night you and your friends terrorized an innocent girl from Colorado to Maine and work through your regret and its aftermath in that fashion. Actually, you can, and you'll still derive the profound benefits of writing. If that is the direction you're being pulled, I encourage you to consider writing memoir instead of fiction.

 The Truth Before Tale exercise in Chapter 2, "Know Thyself," oriented you toward the level of depth and awareness needed to write a novel. This chapter provides the next level of exercises where you transform your ghostly outline of a novel idea that began emerging in that chapter and slap flesh on it.

When it comes to fiction, you can't tweak the surface details and call your experience literature because life doesn't follow the principles of storytelling. Whatever experience you had or person you met that you'd like to confront or revisit through fiction, be prepared to modify them or it to make the novel work. In novelizing your life, you will be using 100 percent of the emotions you felt but only fragments of the actual scenes or people. I mined all of the fear, loss, and shame—there are mountains of shame when your partner kills himself—that follows unexpected death as well as brought in fragments of what I loved and missed about Jay to write my first mystery: the smell of dryer sheets in his flannel shirts, how his lips would quirk when he was about to tell a lie, the love notes he left, how methodically he undertook any task from repainting door trim to writing complex river ecology reports, the argument we had about getting Dairy Queen that was really about how I was terrified of getting married.

However, I could use only what was in service of *May Day*'s larger narrative, a straightforward murder mystery. In so doing, I was able to write a story that I could control, providing closure for me in a situation that offered none on its own. I made peace with the gray areas, explored the emotions from a safe distance, and inoculated myself against the greater grief of Jay's death by creating and playing out a smaller one in novel form.

 My experience in writing May Day *provides a real-life example of how habituation and catharsis, two of the therapeutic modes of fiction writing described in Chapter 1, "The Science of Writing to Heal," work.*

Going through this process was much-needed rehabilitation but also produced good fiction. If I had written the true chronology of Jay's life and death, I could have potentially written about his last day because hyper-traumatic events lend themselves well to narrative, but in the end, that's only twelve hours. The period before and after his suicide was filled with highs and lows but mostly the dull grind of life—worrying about bills, getting a haircut, scrubbing the bathroom grout—which doesn't make good storytelling. Your job as a novelist is to choose experiences that have haunted and resonated with you and then extract the core of those events and spin them into a narrative, not to simply take a day in your life and change the names and locations. It is your epochal events and emotions that are the common language of human experience, and accessing them connects you to something greater and also more elemental than yourself, which has always been the job of fiction.

You must dredge up the foundational emotions and scenes from your life and be prepared to let the rest go. The awareness that you will be repurposing your life rather than merely retelling it gives you permission to excavate the really ugly deposits, places you might otherwise not venture into without the shield and rudder that writing fiction provides. As you undertake this, just remember that you are always in the driver's seat. If you are digging at particularly traumatic memories, don't push too hard. Listen to your instincts.

Let me tell you a story.

I have a friend who was in the first Iraq War. He spent time in a tank on the outskirts of Baghdad. One day, he was on watch at the hatch, gun in hand. There were three other men in the tank with him. They were surrounded by houses, kids playing in the brush. It felt safe, almost like home but not quite, and so my friend had the top of the tank open and was looking around.

As he tells it, a sudden hush came over the village. The families disappeared, and his commanding officer inside the tank received an urgent call. He yelled up to my friend that two snipers had been spotted at the ridge of a nearby hill, and it was my friend's job to shoot them.

He did.

In the middle of their backs, as they ran away, specks on the horizon.

He'd never killed anyone before.

He wept the first time he told me this story. He wondered if maybe they hadn't been snipers at all. Maybe they had been boys playing in the hills. The tank beat a hasty retreat after my friend followed his commander's orders, and so he will never know for sure.

I knew what relief I'd gotten from writing fiction. I asked him if he wanted to use his experience as the basis of a story. He said he'd try.

The first time he wrote about the incident, it came out as sword and sorcery flash fiction, a short story about the ambiguity of combat featuring creatures with only the most passing resemblance to humans. The second time he tackled it, months later, it was a single scene in a coming-of-age novel. The war was Vietnam, not Iraq, and the soldier was on the ground, not in a tank. In this version, the soldier walked up to the two men he'd shot in the back and saw that they were both wired with bombs. By killing them, he'd actually saved his comrades and the innocent villagers.

The speed and direction he took in both fictionalizations was appropriate. Notice how he wasn't able to come at the memory directly at first, and he didn't need to. Both times he wrote about it are an example of inhibition-confrontation, the idea that by fictionalizing your life experiences, you can release the stress associated with suppressing your memories. By working through the emotions of that high-trauma event, he was able to feel a degree of closure on a situation that otherwise didn't offer any and was able to create two powerful pieces of fiction. He didn't rush or force the process. He followed the story, backing off when the discomfort got to be too much and only returning when he could handle it.

Remember this. You're in charge of the writing. Listen to your gut.

Recycling Your Life Experiences

Step 1: Journal

If you're like my friend, or really, like most people, you have a few stand-out moments that are obvious fiction fodder. These are an effective starting point, and likely what you wrote about in the Chapter 2 Truth Before Tale exercise, but they are not enough on their own. You need to expand on them to sustain a novel. If you've already written one or more books, you have a general idea of how to twist a life event into the kernel of a novel concept. That's a good hop-off point, but to create fiction that resonates, that the reader connects with on a profound emotional level, you need to dig below the surface. Both your writing and life will be more powerful if you excavate and reprocess the deeper muck.

Journaling is the best way to do this.

Good thing you have that notebook.

Your job now is to write in it twice a day, ten minutes each time, for seven days, with emotions rather than concepts as your initial writing prompts. Write "Shame" on the top of the page and freewrite every memory, person, song, or thought that comes to mind under that heading. Do the same for "Humor," "Fear," "Sadness," "Anger," "Love," and "Betrayal." Those are archetypal emotions, the ones that sustain a novel. Envision this as writing your emotional resume.

After you've worked through the major emotions, devote a page to "Childhood," and include where and when you were born along with seminal memories. For example, a driving emotion of my child-hood was a sense of spiritual power and connectedness. This is best illustrated in my belief that I knew where buried treasure was (and subsequently dug holes all over our family farm), could sense and talk to ghosts, and had healing powers over plants and animals and so would conduct farm kitty clinics and administer to ferns. If you think these quirks would lend themselves to a young adult novel protagonist, I agree with you, and I never would have remembered them if I hadn't freewritten about childhood memories.

Devote another page to "Regrets" and another to "Aspirations." Once you start digging in those dark caves, prepare for all sorts of memories to burble up. Carry that notebook with you everywhere for at least a week so you have a place to record all your recollections. If you're sleeping, your journal should be next to your bed. If you're out and about, it should be in hand, purse, or backpack. Set your alarm for ten minutes before you need to wake up, and when it goes off, write down all your dreams quick.

RECYCLING YOUR LIFE
EXPERIENCES INTO
NOVEL IDEAS #1

1. Yank out your notebook.

2. Carry it everywhere for a week, freewriting daily. Use these words as freewriting prompts: shame, humor, fear, sadness, anger, love, betrayal, childhood, regrets, and aspirations.

3. In addition to freewriting at least twice a day, ten minutes at a time, write down any memories, images, or emotions that pop up outside the freewriting.

4. Finally, for this week, set your alarm for ten minutes before you normally wake up and write down everything in your head when the alarm goes off.

You won't use all of these ideas in your novel, and since your notebook is your private treasure, don't self-censor. Write down everything, from the name of a childhood best friend to the copper smell of fear that time you were caught shoplifting lilac-colored lipstick to the taste of your first kiss. You've been through a lot. Every one of your inspirations stemming from memories is important at this stage. Tell your secrets to yourself.

It was through this journal-for-a-week process that I remembered Aunt Bea, the daycare lady who locked my sister and me in the closet so her creepy son could perform puppet shows. I also remembered how she tried to feed a three-year-old who'd had an accident his own poop.

After I cleared out that long-hidden memory, a completely unrelated and even more deeply buried image of me at my first college party arose to fill its space, as is common when you're cleaning mental house.

I was still in the small-town-girl-in-a-big-city transition. I'd dyed my hair goth black but still sported claw bangs. I was afraid of everything and felt like I belonged nowhere, and defended myself by being cocky and sarcastic. I'd walked into this party, this stranger's house, like I owned it, and headed straight to the kitchen for liquid courage.

I remember that the Cure was playing.

I was wearing a Jimmy Page t-shirt.

The place was packed, hot bodies crammed into every corner. I was almost to the kitchen when I heard a scream ten feet in front of me. The crowd was parting, miraculously. In seconds, the only thing that stood between me and the keg in the kitchen was a man.

Holding a gun.

Pointed directly at me.

The gun was long, maybe a shotgun, and he held it out with his right arm like we were in a Western.

I didn't know him, had never seen him before, so I don't think he meant to harm me personally. He just had a gun, and he was aiming it, and everyone else was smart enough to get out of the way. Me, I had the strangest reaction, one that still shames me to this day.

I didn't want anyone to think I was scared, so I stayed put.

Time stood still, like it does when you're counting the coins of your life. The party had gone funeral quiet. The gunman and I stared at each other. He was early twenties, sporting a mullet and a trench coat, maybe in the same ugly duckling child-adult stage I was. His eyes were calm. He was sneering. A crowd of fifteen people on either side waited for the situation to end the only way it could.

His trigger finger twitched, but time still didn't move.

I felt myself freezing from the inside out.

Suddenly, he dropped the gun to his side. He took a swig out of his red beer cup. Sound rushed back into the room. The clock started ticking again. The guy next to the gunman laughed, punched his arm. They left through the back door.

I breathed.

The crowd filled in the gun lane, but people maintained a bubble around me.

I found the bathroom, went inside, and cried. I didn't come out until all trace of the redness and tears was gone. I found my friend, who hadn't even come in off the front porch, and told her we had to leave. On the way out, I heard someone retelling the story already. It featured an ugly girl so terrified she couldn't move even with a gun pointed at her forehead.

When that memory made it into my journal, another one appeared, and then another, each lining up like Pez candy once they got the word that I was cleaning my mental garbage pile. Some of the memories that asserted themselves were horrifying, others funny, still others tragicomic, at least to me. For example, I remembered a specific scene from the early '90s, when I worked at an import store on the West Bank of Minneapolis. It was called Global Village. There's still one in Duluth, but I think the Minneapolis one closed for good.

One of my coworkers, Sarah, was a stunning woman. She sported luscious raspberry lips, green eyes, black hair, and a figure like Jessica Rabbit. She was an ethnic chameleon, too smoky to be a Midwesterner, too creamy to be of African descent. Men traipsed in and out of that store in hopes of seeing her. One day, a nice Ethiopian gentleman stopped by. When he found out she was on break, he said he'd wait for her.

It was August, hot as a New Orleans porch. I asked if he wanted to take off his jacket because Sarah wouldn't return for at least twenty minutes.

He balked.

I insisted.

He pulled his jacket tighter.

Because my dubious superpower is cracking dumb jokes in tense situations, I asked him if maybe he didn't want to remove his parka because he was armed.

His eyes widened. He ran out of the store, jacket still on.

When Sarah returned, I told her the story as it had happened, including the name the guy had left me.

Her mouth formed a perfect "O." Then she hooted in laughter. "You asked Abdi if he was armed?"

"Yup." I might have been a little proud.

"He never takes his coat off in public because he's got a prosthetic *arm*."

I am a horrible person.

But that's not really the point. The takeaway is that you can't make this stuff up, and if you journal, you won't have to. That whole scene made it into one of my books, but it's nothing alone. The day before and the day after, a hundred days previous and a hundred days since, are filled with the monotony of life, and life doesn't make good fiction. Scenes, properly ordered, and the jewels of emotion that you will mine in your journal, do. In fact, these authentic feelings and experiences are absolutely essential to crafting compelling fiction.

At the end of the week, if you freewrite twice a day, write down all the memories that knock at your door when you're not freewriting, and set your alarm ten minutes before wake-up time to harvest the memories your subconscious has lined up for you, prepare for new levels of self-awareness as well as fresh, welcome breathing room in your psyche. Cleaning out the past makes room for a new future. As a decided bonus, you will have collected more than enough personal experiences to sustain a novel.

Step 2: Crunch the Letters

After you've devoted a week to mining the rough materials of your memories, the next step is to sift through all the ideas to decide what you want to focus on. At this point, often one or two concepts will be sticking to you and have likely started to populate themselves with characters and scenes. If, however, your core idea is not yet beckoning like a beacon, or more commonly, you have *too* many ideas and don't know which one to choose, I have a handy dandy Novel Idea Table that will help you crunch the letters. It's got a column on the left for your ideas. If you've already uncovered a core idea, or several, write them down in this column, and put a mark in the "Hooks Me" column if it's an idea that is burning up your brain. Then, proceed to fill the appropriate cells to the right in that same row so you have an array of experiences to draw on to flesh out your concept.

If you do not yet have even a snippet of an idea, go about it the opposite way: fill in as many of the cells to the right of the idea column as you can, using each box to bring you closer to your novel idea. Play it like kittywhompus bingo, looking for connected themes vertically, diagonally, horizontally, or piecemeal. Once you create enough connections, you'll have your novel idea.

I've included an example of the Novel Idea Table that I filled out after my most recent week of journaling. After that, I've provided a blank table for your use, followed by an explanation of what goes in each of the columns.

Check it out.

Novel Idea Table: (Example)

Idea	Requirement						Bonus		
	Hooks Me	Experience with Strong Emotional Resonance	Recurring Mistake	Story or Image I Can't Shake	I Wish I Had ___	Recurring Dream	Genre I Read In	Marketable	Contains Character, Setting, Central Conflict, Theme
Eve: Seventeen-year-old Eve Catalain must learn to trust in her own power when she uncovers the terrible secret binding the people of the not-quite-right town of pre-WWI Faith Falls, Minnesota.	X (I want to know how this story ends; supporting ideas keep coming to me)	X Uncovering a terrible secret—Jay's addiction—and responding from fear; Karl's face when I broke up with him—sadness at hurting a kind heart	X Being attracted to men with devastating secrets	X Frog rain, ball of snakes, Queen Anne	X Trust in my own power and worth	X (Waiting on the riverbank, trapped, languid)	X (Lit fiction—gothic suspense)	X Alice Hoffman, Sarah Addison Allen	X C=Eve; S=Faith Falls, MN; CC=solving the mystery of the town; T=claiming one's own power

	X	X	X	X	X		X	X	X
March of Crimes: When budding Battle Lake PI Mira James is discovered in the same room as a human corpse disguised as a life-sized doll, she must flee the law and find the true killer to avoid life in prison.	(I want more levity in my life)	Locked in closet at Aunt Bea's for puppet shows with lifelike dolls; being accused of cheating on tenth grade English test when I hadn't cheated	Not relying on others for help	Life-size homemade dolls sitting at the Hackensack Diner lunch counter	The courage to always speak up for myself, to confront others		(Mystery)	My publisher wants another book in the series	C=Mira; S=Battle Lake, MN; CC=solving the mystery of killer/doll-maker; T=good vs. evil
The Magic of Weaving: Emmy Smith's life unravels when her father commits suicide, uncovering a trail of deception leading back to her childhood.		Jay's suicide—the argument before, chaos after, dealing with police, blood removal, funeral, questions, family, recovery	Being attracted to men with devastating secrets	The sound of his voice after he'd decided to kill himself; brain matter on his glasses; the feel of his cold, dead foot; newlyweds at State Park asking me to take their photo	Answers and full recovery from trauma		(Lit fiction)		C=Emmy; S=Duluth??; CC=rebuilding a life post-trauma; T=personal redemption

RECYCLING YOUR LIFE EXPERIENCES INTO NOVEL IDEAS #2

Use the memories you gathered in your journal to create your own Novel Idea Table.

Novel Idea Table

Idea	Requirement						Bonus	
	Hooks Me	Experience with Strong Emotional Resonance	Recurring Mistake	Story or Image I Can't Shake	I Wish I ___ Had ___	Recurring Dream	Genre I Read In	Marketable · Contains Character, Setting, Central Conflict, Theme

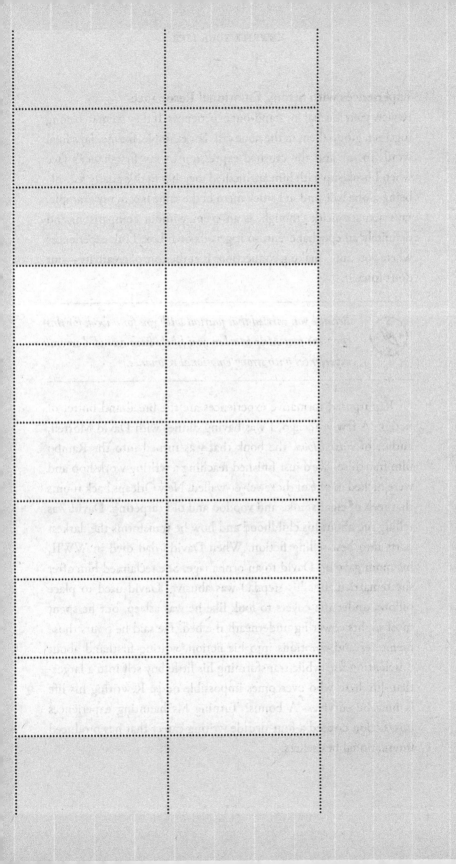

Experiences with Strong Emotional Resonance

Review your journal for stand-out experiences. If they seem to belong together, group them in the same cell. For example, for me, Jay's final words to me and the crushed expression of my first fiancé's face when I broke up with him are meshed together in this gnarly fear-of-being-alone ball, and so I stuck them in the same box in my example. Jay's actual suicide, though, is an event without comparison, and definitely an epochal event, so it gets its own box. Link experiences where you can—making connections is at the core of creativity—but don't force it.

 Because you carried that journal with you for a week for this chapter's first Mile Marker, you likely have recorded several experiences with strong emotional resonance.

Repurposed formative experiences are the bread and butter of fiction. A few years ago, I was having dinner with David Morrell, author of *First Blood*, the book that was turned into the Rambo film franchise. We'd just finished teaching a writing workshop and were tucked in one of those velvet-walled, New Orleans back rooms that reek of cigar smoke and voodoo and old carpeting. David was telling me about his childhood and how he transforms the darkest parts into best-selling fiction. When David's dad died in WWII, his mom gave up David to an orphanage. She reclaimed him after she remarried, but his stepdad was abusive. David used to place pillows under the covers to look like he was asleep, but he spent most nights cowering underneath the bed. He said he pours those memories and emotions into his fiction, writing firsthand about unrelenting fear while transforming his little boy self into a larger-than-life hero who overcomes impossible odds. Rewriting his life is how he survives. A bonus? Turning his haunting experiences into fiction created a four-decade writing career that has produced international bestsellers.

Sylvia Plath's achingly powerful *The Bell Jar* weaves her personal battle with depression into the tapestry of fiction. Ned Vizzini's best-selling *It's Kind of a Funny Story* was inspired by his own psychiatric hospitalization. *The House on Mango Street*, by Sandra Cisneros, contains many scenes sewn together from her richest moments, including her experiences growing up in a diverse neighborhood united by family and poverty, which contributed to a life-long quest to find a home that felt like her own. But remember, you can't simply change the names of the key players or setting and call it fiction, which is why you need to dig deep and make as many connections as you can.

A Recurring Mistake
Ever notice how your life's problems seem to run on a loop, and you face a version of the same situation over and over again until you *finally* choose correctly and are allowed to move on? For me, I spent twenty years of my life dating fixer-uppers. Each time, I'd only see the good and explain away the bad. Exploring that theme through fiction has helped me finally (fingers crossed) land an actual partner. We all have these recurring issues we need to face. I have a friend who continually ended up with men who cheat on her (that friend is me). I have another who, every few years, is fired from a job he likes. Still another friend is perpetually unhappy with her body and swings from one failed diet to another. What bad things keep happening to you over and over again, seemingly without your blessing? Write 'em down.

Story or Image I Can't Shake
This column in the Novel Idea Table doesn't necessarily refer to something that involved you directly; it can be something that you heard about or saw that has rattled you. As such, it becomes your emotional dust, irritating you and clinging to your psyche. These are perfect sources of fiction. For example, Laura Lippman's *What*

the Dead Know is inspired by the real-life, unsolved mystery of twin sisters Sheila and Kate Lyon. Lippman first heard the story when she was sixteen years old. Never able to shake it, she fictionalized the tale thirty years later.

While reading a book about mental disorders, Maud Casey discovered the story of Albert Dadas, a nineteenth century man whose pathology drove him to walk continually. Unable to shake the lyricism and innocence of Dadas' recollections, Casey fictionalized him in her novel, *The Man Who Walked Away*.

The secondhand story or image that haunts you can be obscure. My mother once told me about a couple vacationing in Colorado with their two kids, ages four and six. During a tour of an underground waterfall in Colorado, the four-year-old pulled away for a moment, ducked under the fencing, and toppled into the roaring waterfall where he was brutally and immediately wrenched toward the center of earth, no chance of saving him. That was literally the last time those parents, who loved their kids enough to take them on a family trip and who I imagine to be caring, wholehearted people, ever saw their child. I cannot shake that damn story.

Pull out the stories and images you can't lose, that have gotten under your skin, and ask yourself "what if?" Record them in the Novel Idea Table to see if they've got the legs to sustain a full-length book.

I Wish I Had _____

This prompt is like regrets, but not exactly because you're still alive so you can do something about them. Maybe you wish you had the courage to go back to college at fifty-four, or the ability to captivate a room with your public speaking, or more than anything you wish you had said yes that night the lead singer from the Black Crowes invited you to the back of the tour bus. List the regrets that ping at you or life goals that you secretly or not-so-secretly cling to.

A Recurring Dream

Even if you're not a lucid dreamer, odds are that during your week of journaling, you remembered a persistent dream. I have two. The first I've had every few years since I was four and features little-girl-me crouching next to a bathtub. A man is standing behind me. I can't see him, but his hands are on my shoulders. They are white and papery. He's killed my dad and my sister and literally placed my mother in my hands. She is shrunk to the size of a matchstick, wrapped in linen. He urges me with an eerily kind voice to place her in the bathtub.

I do.

The scariest part of the dream is how compassionate he seems.

He turns on the water. My mom is drowning; I can hear her tiny screams. He hands me a salt shaker and a pepper shaker. If I sprinkle one on her, she'll be saved. If I sprinkle the other, she dies. I don't know which is which.

I wake up just as I'm tipping the salt shaker over her tiny shroud.

You better believe I'm going to puzzle that last one out in a future novel. Not only will it help me clear my psyche, but also exquisitely lucid dreams are the stuff of many great novels, including *Sophie's Choice, Strange Case of Dr. Jekyll and Mr. Hyde, Stuart Little*, and *Frankenstein*.

My second recurring dream burrowed into my sleeping brain when I was twelve. It features me on a riverbank, languid, full, drowsy. I'm playing with friends, but we're all so sleepy. Suddenly, my playmates jump up, screaming with terror and pointing toward the woods. They race into a tower and yell for me to follow them. I can't. I'm too content.

Meanwhile, a monster is coming for me. His crashing footsteps tremble the treetops, but I can't bring myself to run away. I always wake up right before he comes into view, always with the knowledge that he *got me and it was my fault because I didn't move*. That recurring dream became the basis for my first young adult novel. Sift through your journal for recurring dreams of your own, and write them in the appropriate column in your own Novel Idea Table.

# # #

After you've filled out the Novel Idea Table's primary cells as best you can, drawing lines connecting complementary ideas if they didn't naturally fall in the same row, look over what you've noted. If you didn't have ideas percolating before, you have them now. Write them out in your "Idea" column, and check the "Hooks Me" column if it's an idea with some fire. Once you have your ideas written out and have thought about whether or not they hook you, it's time to explore the last three columns in your table. Note that you need something written in at least a couple of the first six columns for your idea to have legs. These last three columns are good to have, but not a requirement.

Genre I Read In

Begin to think what genre each emerging idea would best fit in, reviewing Chapter 4 if you have questions. If you have a gut feeling for what genre would best serve the story or which you would most like to explore, scribble it in this column. Remember that the more you read in a genre, the better equipped you are to write in it.

Marketable

After you decide on a potential genre, do a little research to find out what other books are being published in this genre and if your idea sounds marketable. Whether or not you can sell it shouldn't be your driving force, but for some writers it's a consideration. Search "*New York Times* bestsellers" to analyze descriptions in the genre you're proposing and measure whether yours is in the ballpark. If you have no intention of publishing, feel free to ignore this column.

Contains Character, Setting, Central Conflict, and Theme

Finally, brainstorm a main character, central conflict, setting, and theme. If you think of a concept for a novel as a general dish, say an egg frittata, then character, central conflict, setting, and theme are the eggs, cheese, onions, and salt you need to bake that frittata. Here are examples from the descriptions I provided earlier in this chapter:

Carrie Fisher
Delusions of Grandma

> Main Character: screenwriter Cora Sharpe
>
> Central conflict: she and her mother bust her senile grandfather out of a nursing home
>
> Setting: Hollywood
>
> Theme: learning the meaning of love

Ray Bradbury
Dandelion Wine

> Main Character: twelve-year-old Douglas Spaulding
>
> Central conflict: dealing with death and loss
>
> Setting: a 1928 summer in small-town Illinois
>
> Theme: coming of age

Amy Tan
The Joy Luck Club

> Main Character: Jing-Mei (June) Woo
>
> Central conflict: reconciling a mother/daughter relationship
>
> Setting: San Francisco and China
>
> Theme: the wings and chains of family

In all of these examples, the resultant novel is so much more than these rough sketches—more characters, multiple conflicts, diverse settings, layered themes—but these four elements constitute the core ingredients for baking that novel. The more elements you start with, the stronger your book. Also, the easier it is to write.

To nail these four basic components for your own novel idea, review the information you have so far recorded in your table. Then, complete as many of the following sentences as best as you can:

- The event or conflict I most want to explore is:_____
  _____
  _____
  _____

- The qualities (age, gender, one or two personality traits, name if it comes to you) of the character I most want to experience this event are:_____
  _____
  _____
  _____

- The primary setting that best fits this event is:_____
  _____
  _____
  _____
  _____

- The recurring pattern in my life that I want to break free from is:_____
  _____
  _____

The answers to the preceding questions will give you, in order, your novel's central conflict, main character, setting, and theme.

RECYCLING YOUR LIFE EXPERIENCES INTO NOVEL IDEAS #3

If you do not yet have a fully formed idea for your novel (Column 1 in the Novel Idea Table), then selecting a character, setting, central conflict, and theme are the launch pad that will lead you to the idea.

Here are my answers to those questions so you can see how I created the character, setting, conflict, and theme for *Eve*:

- The event or conflict I most want to explore is: *Uncovering a terrible secret.*

- The qualities (age, gender, one or two personality traits, name if it comes to you) of the character I most want to experience this event are: *I want to go back in time and choose differently, so I want this character to be young (late teens), female, curious, naïve, and unaware of her personal power.*

- The primary setting that best fits this event is: *fictional Minnesota because I know it and can add the necessary sensory detail. Also, it includes the Queen Anne and ball of snakes, which are two stories I can't shake. Finally, that's also where I uncovered a terrible secret, so it'll have the most resonance and authenticity.*

- The recurring pattern in my life that I want to break free from is: *being attracted to men with devastating secrets/ underselling myself.*

I selected literary fiction for my genre, and specifically gothic suspense because I've been reading and loving a lot of it, and so after researching descriptions of other books in that subgenre on Amazon and on the *New York Times* Bestseller List, I crunched my information and came up with this idea for the current novel I'm writing, *Eve,* which I then wrote in the first column of my Novel Idea Table:

> The year is 1907, and seventeen-year-old Eve Catalain has arrived to Faith Falls, Minnesota, along with the quarter-century rising of the snakes. As beautiful and elusive as a firefly, she has captured the eye of Crucifer Darkly and Ennis Patterson equally. Crucifer is wicked and wealthy, the source of dark rumors, respected to his face and feared behind his back. Ennis is twenty years older than Eve, quiet, kind, and wretchedly content to be her friend. When Eve defies Crucifer's command to never enter his mansion at night, she uncovers a secret the town would kill to keep hidden. How she responds will either cement her personal power or curse generations of Catalain women to come.

We'll talk about how to refine an idea and transform it into a book in later chapters. For now, you just need to pick the novel idea that speaks loudest to you. In a perfect world, after you've filled out your Novel Idea Table, you'll find one row has more information and *x*'s than any other, and that's the idea you'll choose. In the real world, however, regardless of how many *x*'s you end up with, one of these ideas is going to go neon for you. That's just how it works, always. Hang on to the other ones. You can use them as subplots, others can be scenes, and still others can be subsumed into a larger idea.

PARTING THOUGHTS ON NOVEL IDEAS

To recap, there is no bad idea—just bad ideas for *you.* The concept you choose for your novel needs to reverberate with you, and you need to dig to find out what that is. Fill in the Novel Idea Table, plus keep your journal close and make room for inspiration. Please notice when it arrives. What are you doing when inspiration lands? Are you hiking, gardening, showering? Can you include this activity in your life more often? After a week of journaling religiously and filling in as much of the Novel Idea Table as you can, you'll discover which concept most needs your love and attention.

Once you've chosen the idea that is going to guide your novel, prepare to release your experiences to a larger narrative. Be willing to add (conflict, characters, epiphanies that you didn't learn until after the event), subtract (shrink the timeline, or the characters, or the backstory), and multiply (assign motives when you may not know what they were, create connections between events and people that weren't obvious in life, amplify the protagonist's inner or outer journey to craft a full character arc for them and a lesser one for your antagonist). The next four chapters will guide you step-by-step through this process of growing a concept into a novel. Right now, celebrate your idea, nurture it, and be prepared to let it propagate.

I'm ending this chapter with two pieces of advice, neither originating from me. The first I heard at a conference, shortly after my first book came out. A panel of best-selling mystery writers was seated at the front of the room. Approximately two hundred aspiring writers sat in the audience. One woman raised her hand and timidly asked whether she should hold off on using all of her good ideas in her first novel because then what would she have left for her second novel.

After some polite laughter, the moderator told her the truth: spend your good ideas now. Your brain will make more. As Maya Angelou said, "You can't use up creativity. The more you use, the more you have." Don't hold back when you journal and definitely get it all out when you write your novel. The more ideas you honor, the more crowd in for that same kind of treatment.

The second piece of advice comes from Elizabeth Gilbert, who was speaking at a retreat I attended. A young author asked Gilbert how she knew which ideas to use when writing *Eat, Pray, Love* and which to leave out. The question wasn't so much about using up all your good stuff as it was about being overwhelmed with potential directions and not knowing how to select what helped the story and what hurt it.

"That's easy," Elizabeth Gilbert said in a way that made everyone believe her. I think that's how she must say everything. She's amazing. "Every book I write, I write to *one* person. It doesn't have to be someone close to me, and they don't ever have to know."

Let this simple truth guide you as you grow your idea. Who most needs to read the book you'll be writing? What parts of the story must they know? What won't matter to them? What tone must you strike? By deciding that, and sticking to it from the brainstorming stage to final edits, you will instinctively know what to include in your novel and what to leave out.

Here's how I know. When I first wrote about the painful, raw truth of Jay's suicide, it was written as an essay to the first man I seriously dated after Jay's death. It had been eight years. I was scared, I was raising two small kids, and I was geographically isolated, but I knew that I didn't want to be alone any longer.

When I met Dale,[1] I thought I'd found everything. He was an artist, a writer, a great lover, funny. I discovered four years into the relationship that he was also unfaithful and that he was never going to be anything but inexplicably angry with life. Still, in that pocket between finding out he'd cheated and realizing my kids and I would be better off without him, I needed him to know how badly he'd hurt me.

So, for the first time in my life, I wrote the true story of my experience with Jay's suicide. Like a surgeon, I cut out the details that would distract or bore Dale. I kept the words spare and lean and let the story speak for itself. Because I was writing to one very specific

---

[1] I'm going to call him Dale here, to protect the guilty.

person rather than a faceless audience, it's one of the best pieces I've ever written. It hits on every note I want it to. That piece is the introduction to this book.

A side note for any of you who may doubt karma. Two summers after Dale and I split, I received a phone call from an unknown number. I was in the passenger seat of a rental car, traveling to Indiana to teach at a writing conference. Through a wonderful confluence of events, one of my favorite writers in the world, William Kent Krueger, was driving the rental. I answered the phone. A private detective was on the other end of the line. Seems Dale was applying for a high-security government job and the PI needed to call anyone Dale had had a relationship with in the past ten years as a character reference.

Ah.

Choose an idea that speaks to you, one that is borne of personal experience and authentic emotion; flesh it out so you know who the main character is, where it will take place, what the central conflict is, and its theme; use every single good idea that comes to you; and plan on writing this book to one person. Carry that powerful potion forward to the next four chapters, where I'm going to show you, step-by-step, how to transform it into a novel that heals.

Chunk.

Everything is going to fall into place.

CHAPTER 6

CRAFT COMPELLING CHARACTERS

When you ask yourself what a certain character will do given a certain set of circumstances, you're making the decision based on what you yourself would (or, in the case of a bad guy, wouldn't) do. Added to these versions of yourself are the character traits, both lovely and unlovely, which you observe in others. There is also a wonderful third element: pure blue-sky imagination.

—Stephen King

People in a novel, not skillfully constructed characters, must be projected from the writer's assimilated experience, from his knowledge, from his head, from his heart, and from all there is of him.

—Ernest Hemingway

I'm all of my characters. And I'm none of my characters. I can write a truth only if I get out of the way and disappear. And from this Houdini trick, amazingly enough, I reappear.

—Sandra Cisneros

The American Book Award–winning poet Jimmy Santiago Baca tells a story about teaching a writing workshop on the Iron Range, a bleak cut of northern Minnesota populated with hard-scrabble miners. The sexual harassment in this male-dominated, culturally isolated part of the world is legendary. In fact, it's the inspiration for the Charlize Theron film *North Country* about the first successful class action sexual harassment lawsuit in the United States.

Baca is well known for bringing writing workshops to the underserved, and he'd brought this one to the Iron Range. A female miner approached him after he was done teaching. As he tells the story, she asked if she could speak to him alone.

He said yes.

After the other people cleared out, she told him about her first day working in the mines. She grew agitated as she spoke. She had to get the story out, which is why she'd come to the workshop in the first place.

She told Baca she hadn't wanted to take the mining job, she knew how bad it was for women there, but she had children to feed and bills to pay. When she showed up for her first day of work, her locker was papered with pornographic images, she was leered at, men called her names, her work tools were hidden. She was scared, but she didn't leave.

The bills. The children.

Instead, she went into the dark mines with all the men.

It was okay at first. She was learning the job. The other men left her alone to do theirs. When it was time for a lunch break, her supervisor asked her to run to a back room to grab a piece of equipment for him before she ate. She obliged.

The room was dark and big, a single bare bulb dangling from the ceiling, not enough to light the corners but enough to show there wasn't anything but garbage scattered around. This wasn't an equipment room. She realized as soon as she stepped in what was happening, but it was too late.

The biggest man on the team had followed her. He blocked the door. He smiled. "I drew the long straw."

He began walking toward her. The only exit was behind him, and he was huge, too big to slip past. She did the only thing she could think of: she took off her helmet and used it to smash the bare bulb.

The room went black, so dark that her eyes tried to make shapes out of the ink.

"What's your name?" she asked. She was surprised at how steady her voice sounded.

Caught off guard, he told her. Then she told him hers.

"I have two kids," she said. "I wanted to go to college but ended up here. I'm afraid of the dark."

She could hear his breathing five feet in front of her, barely, over the blood thumping of her own heart. He hadn't moved since she'd started talking. "What are you afraid of?" she asked. Her voice wasn't so steady anymore.

But then he told her.

He'd come to rape her, but the darkness had stripped away his perceptions and so his plans. In the dark, she wasn't a threat to his job, a target for his anger, a dare from his coworkers. She was a mom. She was afraid. She was Eleanor. Confronted with her humanity, he shared his own.

As Baca tells it, that's our job as writers, to strip away the artifice and expectations of life and talk to the world in the dark. Honestly. Authentically. With vulnerability and fear and hope. This is nowhere more important than when you're crafting the people who will populate your novel. The motivations and desires of your characters drive your story and are the engine of your personal transformation. Crafting believable and compelling fictional characters turbo boosts real-life empathy and strengthens social skills as well as coping mechanisms because it guides the writer to consider other people's motives and desires, the consequences of choice and of action, and the complexity of life.

WHERE TO FIND THE CHARACTERS

Fictional characters usually come to their writers from one of four sources:

- A concept
- Inspiration from the outside world
- Real people
- The subconscious

Most complex fictional characters are drawn from all four wells, but I've divided them here for clarity.

Characters from a Concept

Sometimes, you have a concept for a novel before you have the characters who will populate it. Take, for example, my first thriller *Salem's Cipher*. The inspiration for the book was threefold. First, I wanted to explore through fiction the ramifications of a child's parent committing suicide. Second, like most people, I spend a lot of time worrying about saying the wrong thing, ruining everything, and generally not fitting in. I wanted to explore that in my fiction in the hopes of releasing some of it. Third and finally, I love puzzles. My brain snaps and pops like a mad dancer when it gets a chance to crack a code, solve a riddle, discover a treasure. I wanted to create a book like a playground for minds like mine.

Salem's Cipher is the result. I had the book's concept before I had the main character. Once I knew what I wanted to write about, I asked what kind of woman would be at the center of this story. She had to be smart, imperfect, and real, with a reason to solve puzzles. Meet Salem Wiley, genius cryptanalyst and reluctant heroine of the series. You learn early in the book that Salem's father killed himself, she feels responsible, and she's been agoraphobic ever since. I also dumped all my social fears into Salem so I could figure out how to overcome them. Finally, I made her a cryptanalyst to feed my hummingbird brain.

If you've developed the concept for your novel before you've discovered the characters, ask yourself who can best carry the story you want to tell.

Inspiration from the Outside World

Our brains like to make connections, and if we pay attention, there is inspiration everywhere: in nature, in visual art, in movies and other books, in song, in history. Toni Morrison was inspired—both in concept and character—to write the powerful antislavery novel *Beloved* after reading two articles about Margaret Garner, a slave who escaped the South with her children in 1856. When the slave hunters tracked down Garner in Ohio, she killed her baby girl rather than let her return to a life of slavery.

J. R. R. Tolkien's hobbits—their simplicity and responsibility to nature—were inspired by the English countryside he grew up in when he asked himself what sort of creatures would best fit the green rolling hills. In a less literary example, writer Kevin Eastman, cocreator of *The Teenage Mutant Ninja Turtles* comic books, was inspired to create the series' legendary antagonist, Master Shredder, while washing dishes. Eastman had accidentally thrust his arm into a box cheese grater. Grabbing the handle, he lifted the soapy grater in the air, imagining a bad guy with graters on each hand. *Think of the damage it could do*, he thought to himself, building the character from that inspiration.

The world around us is a constant source of character ideas, which is yet another reason to carry your journal everywhere you go. You never know when inspiration will leap into your path.

Real People

When I refer to characters inspired by real people, I mean real people in our lives, people we know in at least a passing way, including ourselves. This is far and away the most fertile source of character ideas. J. K. Rowling based Professor Severus Snape on one of her own instructors, "a short-tempered chemistry teacher with long hair . . .

[and a] gloomy, malodorous laboratory." Harper Lee's Dill, Scout's best friend in *To Kill a Mockingbird*, is built almost entirely from Lee's interactions with Truman Capote, her childhood best friend. According to Capote, he and Lee were thick as thieves growing up. Because Lee's father was a lawyer, just like Scout's, Capote and Lee spent their summer afternoons attending trials rather than movies. *On the Road*, Jack Kerouac's quintessential American story, is populated by fictional versions of his Beat Generation friends: Allen Ginsberg, William S. Burroughs, and Neal Cassady.

The people we run with provide rich fodder for our fictional characters, though they always need to be a composite of the people we know. Real humans are inconsistent; fictional characters must behave steadily. So, while it might be perfectly appropriate for you to wake up cranky some days and with a smile on your face others, your character must consistently do one or the other, unless you are portraying someone with mental health issues, or the character's mood change is precipitated by an event in the story. This is true of all characters in your novel. They must behave predictably, which is impossible if we shove a person we know into our novel rather than swiping some of their qualities to sew a patchwork quilt of a character.

Note that when I say they must behave predictably, I don't mean they should be boring. What I mean is that when your character initially appears on the page, you have made a contract with your reader that all the actions and the thoughts of this character will be true. If the character has hidden qualities that you'll reveal later, such as being a murderer or a werewolf or a spy, you have to provide a hint of that when introducing that character. Think of it like a blueprint for a two-bedroom house. If you indicate at the outset that you may be adding on, you are free to do so later. But you can't change the entire floor plan once you've built the character. So, put a pin in qualities and motivations you want to reveal later, which can be as simple as the character laughing uncomfortably loud at a joke, or weirdly avoiding going outside during a full moon, just enough to cue your reader that all isn't as it seems.

Creating composites not only allows us to craft characters who fit the story rather than marionettes that we try to force into a narrative, but also alleviates the fear that we will accidentally offend others by writing about them. Though, it's a strange truth that people never see themselves in the fictional characters they have inspired. Playwright and novelist Craig Johnson provides the best example of this. Craig is the *New York Times* best-selling author of the Longmire books, inspiration for the popular TV show of the same name, and the best storyteller you'll ever hear, bar none. He's old school and has every beat down pat. A few years back at a writing conference, he and I were talking about his first Longmire book, *The Cold Dish*. The book debuts Walt Longmire, the grizzled sheriff of Wyoming's Absaroka County. Longmire is an everyday hero straight out of the best of the Old West, contradictory, imperfect, rich with integrity. He has a conflicted relationship with his father, whom he clearly loves but doesn't always see eye to eye with.

As Craig tells it, he sent an advance copy of *The Cold Dish* to his brother and his father because he was worried. He'd put a lot of his dad's qualities into Longmire's father. He didn't want his father to be mad, or worse, hurt.

Craig's brother called him up *immediately* after reading the manuscript and validated Craig's worst fears. "Craig, I love the book," he said. "Couldn't put it down. But what are you gonna do when Dad reads it? He won't like that you turned him into Longmire's father."

Craig didn't know what he was gonna do. The book was written. It was going into publication.

When his father called later that night, Craig picked up the phone with trepidation.

"I read the book," his dad started. Then he paused. "I like that it's in Wyoming. You do that good. I like the mystery, too. But—"

Here it comes, Craig thought.

"—you didn't get me exactly right in that Sheriff Longmire fellow. Here's where you went off the wrong direction . . ."

Craig didn't hear the specifics. He was too busy realizing that his father had assumed he had inspired the main character, not the main character's dad.

This is not an isolated occurrence. Take parts of the people in your life to create a composite character and piece them together in a way that serves the story, making sure to use fictional names, and those people will never recognize themselves. Chicago mystery writer Barb D'Amato offers my favorite rule of thumb in this area: "the more accurately you portray an asshole in fiction, the less likely they'll recognize themselves." If you're *still* worried about your inspirations recognizing themselves in your fictional characters, there's always writer Elaine Viets' truism: "if you're creating a character based on a real guy, write him with a small penis. No man will ever claim him."

Don't just call on the loud, larger-than-life people you've encountered when creating characters, either. Quiet people are oftentimes more interesting, whether it's Philip, the boy who stole a kiss in kindergarten while you were wearing your favorite white winter hat with the pom poms, or your roommate for only a week in college who answered the dorm phone, "Welcome to Roadkill Café. You kill it, we grill it."

I have one of those quiet people I still want to work in a novel. Her name is Linda. We worked together at the Spicer Dairy Queen when I was in tenth grade. Linda seemed impossibly old at the time but was probably in her late thirties. She hadn't yet made manager and would try to pick up extra hours so she could afford name-brand saltines, which her husband loved but which they could rarely afford with both of them working minimum-wage jobs.

At the time, I was dating the fry cook, a moon-faced boy who always glanced down when he smiled. The DQ and a mutual desire to grind up against someone in the backseat of a car were all that brought us together, and by the end of the summer, I was gearing up to break up with him when Linda took me aside, her eyes huge behind her owly glasses, her home perm framing her face with the precision of Lego hair. She told me that I better hang onto the fry cook because there's a lot worse out there.

There's a lot worse out there.

There was so much sadness packed in that two-minute interaction. Even sixteen-year-old me knew I was looking at a life wasted, one of fear chosen over hope. *There's a lot worse out there.* Can you feel how lonely Linda was? I still can, and that's why she's going to for sure show up in a future book.

Creating composites of people who have hurt you is another option and provides a recipe for powerful fictional characters because they will be born of strong emotions. They say that mystery writers are the nicest people because we get our murderous revenge out on paper, and I think there's something to that. But go gently when you tug at the people associated with your past trauma or stressors. I learned this firsthand when I wanted to write more directly about Jay's suicide—not memoir, but a novel about a woman whose husband commits suicide. It took over a decade for me to approach the story willingly and honestly. As research, I pulled up Jay's obituary, which was still archived online. I thought time would have created a sturdier cushion, but reading the facts of his life brought back the same gray emotions, something like shame, something like terror, both emotions held together by a mean, cloudy fascia. Dredging strong emotions and memories into the light is like pulling monsters from a hole. They pinch and claw and slime. You'll want to drop them more than anything. Your instincts will scream at you to let go. You get to decide if it's too soon to pull them out or if you're ready to herd them into the light so you can finally release them.

The Subconscious

Our brains are always working, even when we're asleep, and dreams are the best way to access that treasure trove of characters, not to mention story ideas. If you get in the habit of sleeping with your journal next to your bed and of setting your alarm for ten minutes earlier than you usually get up, you'll surprise yourself by the dreams you're inhabiting when you awake.

For those of you who are lucid dreamers, or who have a few strong nightmares that really stand out to you, consider mining those for character ideas. The first *Terminator* film is one of my favorite science fiction movies. The idea for the film came to James Cameron in a nightmare. He was working on a film in Italy and was awoken one night from a horrible dream. A metal skeleton had emerged from an explosion and was pulling itself toward Cameron using knives. He scribbled down the image on hotel stationery, and the rest of the story ideas came rushing in. If you're a lucid dreamer, you have some of those images yourself. Look them over and see what you can use.

CHARACTER BUILDING #1: WHAT TO DO WITH THE CHARACTERS ONCE YOU FIND THEM

Your characters may come to you roughly at first, or fully fleshed out, but once you open the gates, trust me that they will come to you. Start asking yourself questions about them—what kind of music they like to listen to, how they behave under pressure, and most importantly, what about them makes you want to spend the next year with them? Is it a rich inner life? Their contradictions? Their sense of adventure or humor?

When you believe you've got a solid idea of who will be your protagonist and who will be the antagonist of your novel, it's time to start your character bible. A character bible is simply character sketches for every major character in a novel, kept all in one place. I recommend using your notebook and devoting no more than two pages each to the protagonist and the antagonist. Provide this information for both of them:

- What's your name? Nickname?

- Anyone ever tell you that you look like someone famous?

- Of all your qualities, which are you most proud of? Where do you think you acquired this quality?

- What do people seem to like the least about you? How does this make you feel?

- What habit of yours would you most like to change?

- If someone looked in your bathroom garbage right now, what would they find? How about your refrigerator?

- What scent do you enjoy the most, and what does it remind you of?

- If you could go back in time and change one day of your life, what day would it be, and why?

- Who do you love most in the world and why?

- What scares you?

- What do you want more than anything? What challenges do you have to overcome to reach/acquire it?

This questionnaire is usually easier to fill out for the protagonist because as writers, we normally identify most with our main character. That's why we've made them the center of the story, after all. But it's crucial that you also know the antagonist because underwritten "opposers" don't allow the protagonist to fully develop and, therefore, result in a flat book. In addition, for those of you considering publishing, a well-written, believable, and sympathetic antagonist can spell the difference between a toss-away novel and a cinematic one. Think Hannibal Lecter in *Silence of the Lambs* and Rhett Butler in *Gone with the Wind* as examples of well-crafted antagonists.

Also—and this is crucial—the same muscle you use to craft a well-rounded antagonist is the one you use to empathize with and forgive yourself and others. Note that forgiveness is not the same as condoning mistreatment or allowing it to continue. It's about choosing to focus your mental energy on what serves you and releasing what doesn't. Lewis B. Smedes' quote is my favorite on the topic: "To forgive is to set a prisoner free and discover that the prisoner was you." That is, unless I'm feeling petty, in which case only Oscar Wilde's quote will do: "Always forgive your enemies—nothing annoys them so much." In either case, exploring the motivations of the nonheroes is important work in terms of learning to accept our own shortcomings as well as those of others.

Novel writing is a healthy place to practice flexing your forgiveness muscle so you can use it wisely and happily in your real life. So, make sure you know your antagonist as well as your protagonist, and remember that the villain is the hero of her own story.

 We'll cover how to intersect character with plot in Chapter 7, "Structure Your Story," and how to weave it into a novel in Chapter 9, "Pull It All Together," but for now, just focus on developing your protagonist and your antagonist, making sure both fit into the concept you've developed, and if they don't, altering either the concept or characters as needed.

As you develop these two pivotal characters, watch out for the following potholes. They can't be stereotypes, like the gruff detective or the orphaned princess or the prostitute with a heart of gold. Create real people rather than a list of qualities.

In that same vein, avoid creating Mary Sues—annoyingly perfect, fictionalized versions of ourselves. Characters need to be flawed. Achieving this layering is easiest if you remember that it's your job as a writer to follow, not lead, your characters through the story. Former President

Jimmy Carter was asked during an NPR interview what was the most surprising part of writing *The Hornet's Nest*, his only work of fiction. Carter said that moment came when he wanted one of his characters to be faithful to his wife, but the character kept cheating. That's the sign of good instincts—a writer who wants to go one way but instead listens to the wishes and duties of the character and story. Prepare to be surprised by where your characters take the story—and you.

Along those same lines, the characters you create cannot be flat. They must have an arc. In other words, they must be different in some way at the end of the story than they were at the beginning. Also, every character who appears in your novel must add something to the narrative. You won't have to worry about this requirement with the protagonist and antagonist, as they are the headliners, but keep it in mind as you begin to develop supporting characters.

Let's pause for a simple, shorthand reminder: at its most basic, a novel says "no" to the main character. Repeatedly. Decide what your protagonist wants more than anything and throw ever-larger obstacles in their path until they either reach their goal or realize that they had a different goal all along. Within that framework, only include supporting characters who either help or inhibit your protagonist from reaching that goal.

Finally, when creating your characters, remember that you've got to feel something as you write. If your character is devastated, plan on being saddened, too. If they are jubilant, you are elated as you write that scene. Gustav Flaubert once said of penning *Madame Bovary*, "The taste of arsenic was so real in my mouth when I described how Emma Bovary was poisoned, that . . . I vomited my dinner." While I don't advocate this level of discomfort, it's crucial to crafting compelling characters that you feel their emotions. It works like an inoculation. Little doses call up your resources. You produce antibodies. You fight the invader. You heal, and you grow strong. Your fictional characters will be the golems of Jewish folklore, living creatures created from mud to take on your fears and hopes and lighten your load.

This chapter has been devoted to helping you to craft your own powerful fictional characters. Here is an exercise designed to give you models of how those characters can come to life within a successful narrative.

CHARACTER BUILDING #2

For this leg of your novel-writing journey, you're going to make visible the hidden elements of characterization by watching three films. While movies and novels are not identical, they have a lot of crossover in their structure. I've chosen two of the films for you—*The Color Purple* and *Chinatown*—because they offer some of the most memorable, poignant, and finely sketched characters in cinematic history. You will choose the third film; make sure it is a film in the genre you are considering writing your novel in.

Have a pen handy so you can sketch notes about anything you learn about character development as you watch, paying particular attention to how you are first introduced to the protagonist and antagonist, how you are asked to empathize with them, their strongest personality traits, main goals, main obstacles, fears, the manner of their evolution or devolution, and how you feel about them and why. Your goal in taking these notes is to pull back the curtain on what makes for a nuanced, compelling fictional character so you can employ those qualities in your own writing. If you prefer a table to guide your note-taking as you view the films, please refer to Appendix B.

CHAPTER 7

STRUCTURE YOUR STORY

Let us define plot. We have defined a story as a narrative of events arranged in their time-sequence. A plot is also a narrative of events, the emphasis falling on causality. "The king died and then the queen died," is a story. "The king died, and then the queen died of grief," is a plot. The time-sequence is preserved, but the sense of causality overshadows it. Or again: "The queen died, no one knew why, until it was discovered that it was through grief at the death of the king." This is a plot with a mystery in it . . .

—*E. M. Forster*

It's not how the detective works on the case. It's how the case works on the detective.

—*Joseph Wambaugh*

There is only one plot—things are not what they seem.

—*Jim Thompson*

Tell me the most embarrassing thing that has ever happened to you.

What? You'd prefer if I went first? You goofball.

I'd *love* to.

The year is 1984. I am fourteen, a shaver is my preferred eyebrow-grooming tool, and to ensure that my perm does not so much as lift on the breeze, I spray my hair with Aqua Net while curling it with a hot, thick-barreled iron.

At the moment relevant to this story, I'm wearing a leotard.

In public.

By choice.

It is a Tuesday afternoon in November. I'm in gymnastics practice, and because Paynesville High School is small, the gymnasts are sharing the gym with the wrestlers. I have a crush on Manly Wilder,[1] who wrestles at 138 and is on the other side of the gym, ironically also wearing a leotard. (They called it a unitard. No one was fooled.)

I am *sure* he doesn't know I'm about to take a practice go at the vault, but he might catch a glimpse at my magnificence by chance. Right? He might. And so I perk up on my toes, like I'd seen gymnasts do on TV, and I take off at a brisk pace toward the springboard, hands Barbie-stiff as I run because I'd also witnessed a professional gymnast do that.

I hit the springboard. *Sproing.*

I am sailing. My hands land on the cool leather vault just right, my feet pointed sharply to each side, and I am cruising, a gazelle, but one that can fly. I am almost over the vault. The huge Port-a-Pit zooms toward me, beckoning, its green face offering a soft, safe landing. I know I can fall into it in a big messy bundle and be okay, but I want to do better than that.

I want to land on my feet. Standing up.

Like a pro.

Because, you know, Manly Wilder.

I tuck my knees under me, but my right hand hasn't left the vault. I have thrown off my trajectory.

It's too late to correct. I am tumbling, right hand twisted on the vault, left hand gallantly attempting to facilitate hitchhiking away from what is about to happen, my legs a Pig-Pen ball of dirty confusion up around my head.

---

[1] Not his real name.

I am a mess. Scientifically, it's not even possible what my body is doing.

Rather than land on my feet, I am about to land on my face.

And—because why go half-dumbass?—my mouth is open and I'm shrieking.

KaBLAM.

I hit the mat mouth first. At first, I think it's not so bad. The cushion that has caught me is three feet thick. Except for a little facial road rash, I'm not hurt. Except, why can't I feel my mouth? Hold that. Why can't I *move my head?*

A quick body scan accompanied by pure humiliation and the wet-penny taste of blood reveals what has happened. Turns out that when you hit a Port-a-Pit face-first with your mouth open, wearing a white-chevroned green leotard and traveling at a speed of two to seven miles per hour, the only possible result is that you will power-floss your teeth with the thick plastic threads that make up the mat's woven surface. Physics, you fickle rascal.

The threads are embedded deep in my mouth.

The mat has literally lassoed me to it by my teeth, a big dumb Gulliver in a green leotard.

I stretch a little. Probably Manly has seen me, sure, but if I play it cool like I'm super-relaxed and want to hang on this big pillow of a gymnastics mat, face-really, really-first, I can buy myself time to figure out how to dis-embed the green threads from my incisors and release myself.

"Jessie! Off the mat. Lisa's up next."

Christ on a cracker.

Drool is beginning to pool below my face, something that happens when you can't close your mouth. Footsteps are hammering close. There isn't time.

I place a hand on each side of my head and yank my melon free.

I am willing to sacrifice teeth to avoid explaining this. Forget willing. I *race* to trade emotional pain for physical.

Against all odds, my chew-my-foot-off-quality plan works. The yank has set me free. I glance wildly toward the wrestling mat. People are staring at me. My coach is running in my direction. I am sure I appear like some crazy bird pretending to be human. I race to the bathroom, hands over my mouth. My tongue is numb, I have red crisscrosses over the lower half of my face, and a little pool of blood has gathered behind my lower teeth. But I am free, *thank god, I am free*. Also, I am not leaving this bathroom until all the marks are gone and I have some story (lie) to explain what just happened.

Good times, right? I am the protagonist in that story, the Port-a-Pit is the antagonist (and possibly also my coach, who could have done a girl a large and not called her out when she was power-flossing with a mat), and the setting is the Paynesville High School gym.

Everything else is plot.

Life, in many ways, is plot.

But here's where it gets tricky to convert facts into fiction: most of our lives are boring. They don't make good stories even when we've lived through dramatic events. You will definitely be able to pull out an encounter here or a moment there that would make a good scene, but the disorder of our lives does not lend itself to narrative.

It's troubling at first to realize that our life events in the order they happened will never make good fiction. That's what many people who attend my writing workshops want to turn into a book—"this happened to me, and then this happened, and then this, and it was unbelievable!" While those experiences won't make good fiction in their given state, the good news is that you still have the right stuff to craft a compelling story. It's what you've *learned* from your life events and what you want more than anything that drive the plot, not the events themselves.

Let me first briefly cover the mechanics of plot before showing you how you can distill your own experiences to create an original and compelling plot for your novel.

We'll start at the beginning. The gold standard definition of plot comes from fourth century BCE philosopher Aristotle, who believed plot, or what he called the sequence of events, was the most important component of a drama, even more important than the characters.

He believed that the events must be related to each other, and more than anything, that the plot must arouse emotion in the audience.

He broke plot structure into three acts, coinciding with the audience need for intermission. The first act includes the story setup, popularly referred to as the "inciting incident." The stakes continue to rise in the second act and include a false victory, that point where you think the story is over but it turns out it's not. The false victory is referred to as a major reversal because the trajectory of the story reverses. The climax comes in the third act, followed by the denouement, a French word meaning "to untie," which perfectly describes the cleaning up of any loose ends that happens at the end of a narrative.

The first *Star Wars* movie is a great example of Aristotle's three-act structure in action. The inciting incident occurs when Luke's aunt and uncle are killed, which pushes him to leave the planet with Obi-Wan and sets the story in motion. The stakes rise in the second act when Luke rescues Princess Leia but loses Obi-Wan. The false victory comes when Luke, Leia, and Han escape the Death Star, but it's not over yet. Darth Vader is gathering power and knows where the rebels are hiding. Luke destroying the Death Star with his one-in-a-billion shot is the climax, and the denouement is the awards ceremony at the end of the film.

Inciting incident. Rising stakes. False victory. Denouement.

In the late 1800s, a German writer, Gustav Freytag, came up with a modification of Aristotle's model. (Because those with German blood are controlling and can never leave well enough alone; at least that's what my first live-in boyfriend told me. Coincidentally, my ancestors on my mom's side are from Germany.) Freytag's main changes were to allow for more setup of the main character's motivation in the beginning and to put the climax at the dead middle, which gives as much time to the untying at the end as to the setting up at the beginning.

The film version of *The Wizard of Oz* is the standard example for this model of storytelling. We learn about Dorothy's dissatisfaction at home, much as we learn of Luke's in the beginning of *Star Wars*, but Dorothy has the added motivation of needing to save Toto from being euthanized, escaping an incoming tornado, and squishing the Wicked Witch of the East, all of which weight the front end of *The Wizard of Oz* more heavily than was *Star Wars'* first act. In addition, *The Wizard of Oz* climax appears in the dead center when Dorothy melts the Wicked Witch. There is still the Wizard to deal with, and the Scarecrow's brain, the Lion's courage, and the Tin Man's heart to acquire, as well as Dorothy to get home, which counterbalances the longer beginning. So, where Aristotle's three-act structure is more of a steadily rising line with a sharp drop at the end, Freytag's structure can be visualized as a triangle with no bottom.

Both Aristotle and Freytag's methods of organizing plot have remained the standard bearers, with few alterations, until the 1960s when mythologist Joseph Campbell began to gain an audience for his theories of the hero's journey. According to Campbell, stories are not only the binding agents of culture but also what binds our souls to our bodies.

In other words, humans need stories to survive.

Campbell went on to say—pulling in an impressive library of examples—that every myth, whether scratched on a cave wall or uttered by a holy priest or typed by a college freshman, comes down to one basic structure, or plot: the transformation of consciousness via trials. He broke this transformation into three steps, or acts: departure, fulfillment, and return.

Every single story, from the prehistoric to the biblical to the modern.

Departure. Fulfillment. Return.

I do love the elegance of Campbell's model, as well as the universality. So did and do many. You'll recognize this departure-fulfillment-return structure in many movies, including *The Matrix, O Brother Where Art Thou, The NeverEnding Story*, and *Lion King*. I also appreciate Aristotle's point about plot needing to affect the reader and scenes needing to be causal rather than episodic, and damn if most compelling narratives can't be broken down into a three-act structure. And Freytag is right on the money when he points out that we need to feel an emotional connection at the beginning of the story.

But on the whole? Don't feel married to anything you just learned about the academic models of story structure. The only reason I even mention them is that they might come up in a conversation, and I want you to sound smart. Some other words that are good for that are "schadenfreude," "epitome," "pulchritude" (it doesn't mean what you think), and "recalcitrance." But actually trying to follow one of the academic models of narrative structure feels like donning a crown and elbow gloves to dig a ditch. Real writing, in my experience, is blue collar work, and that's all there is to it. You have to dive into the heart of yourself and subsequently your characters, uncover what they want *more than anything*, throw obstacles—like life has done to you—into their paths, and follow them as they overcome them (or not) and get closer (and sometimes farther) from their goals. Every event has to lead directly to another event—it's a cause-and-effect daisy chain.

It's not just me who believes that the key to good plotting is to figure out what your character wants and follow them. Scratch a writer, and you'll find out that very few of them use one of the classic structures when they craft. Writing professor Matthew Jockers conducted an interesting study that stylishly illustrates this point. Jockers designed a computer program that charts the emotional silhouette, or plot, of any book.

Jockers used best-selling novels for his study, including *The Secret Life of Bees, The Lovely Bones, Gone Girl, All the Light We Cannot See, The Da Vinci Code,* and *The Notebook.* When he programmed the narrative arc for each of these novels into his computer program, it spit out lovely data that resembles the spiky, random readouts you see in a heartbeat monitor. In other words, the plots of these best-selling novels have nothing in common—no clean three-act structure, no triangle without a bottom. Most novels do not follow the classic models. They adhere to their own internal pulse.

Turns out there is only one universal rule of plot, and it goes back to what Joseph Campbell uncovered: every single story worth telling is about transformation via trials. There is no pattern to that because each character's evolution is as unique and as individual as your transformation or mine.

So, the good news—and the bad news—is that there is no one-size-fits-all *formula* for plot. The only certainty is that your character must somehow depart from their regular life to seek out what they want more than anything (love, justice, understanding, etc.), undergo transformative trials, and return to a different life than they lived before.

This is beautiful, right? Crafting plot is where the real transformation of self begins, and where the blood-and-guts of writing gets a test drive. You already have an idea of your genre, your novel idea, and your protagonist and antagonist. The next step is to decide what your protagonist wants more than anything, to throw obstacles into their path, and to follow them through their transformation. And you're going to make sure that what your protagonist wants is also what you want so that you can put the authenticity and energy into it that best-selling fiction requires. A Map exercise at the end of the chapter will guide you with this step.

Also, when you're choosing a goal for your protagonist and subsequently structuring your story, it might be helpful to know while there isn't a formula for plot, there are some hard-and-fast rules:

- Begin your story as close to the end as possible, to paraphrase Kurt Vonnegut. Dive right into the heart of it and start unpacking. The same is true of scenes, which are the building blocks of plot. Start a scene as close to the end as possible, and end it as early as you can.

- The opening of the book must establish an emotional connection with the protagonist. The poignancy doesn't need to happen on page one, and the character doesn't need to (and shouldn't) be a saint, but readers need to feel something for them. In screenwriting, this is called saving the cat. The protagonist can yell at old ladies, steal from a blind man's cup, and cheat at cards, as long as they go out of their way to save one creature from discomfort. Start watching for it in movies. You'll find that in the first ten minutes, the lead character will enact some version of saving a cat.

- The novel's opening (somewhere in the first five chapters) must establish what your protagonist wants more than anything.

- The rest of the novel should consist of a series of trials and conflicts, keeping the protagonist from reaching their goal, snatching away victories. These trials cannot be episodic. In other words, they can't be of equal value, one after the other—first, your protagonist encounters a lion, then a bear, then a flood. The trials must instead be somehow connected, one inextricably leading to another, with ever-increasing stakes. First, your protagonist encounters a lion, then hides in a cave to escape and discovers a bear, but can't leave through the rear of the cave because there is a flood and can't dash out the cave's mouth because there's a hungry lioness crouching nearby, so they are forced to escape through a hole in the cave's roof, where they discover a world they never knew existed. Every action must have a consequence, must be necessary. You're weaving a chain, and if some action isn't a result of something that happened before it and doesn't affect what comes after it, it doesn't belong.

- The character needs to reach a point where all seems lost.

- The character needs to end the story with a different consciousness than they began it, and most of the loose ends must be tied up.

That's it. The rest of the narrative is your canvas to explore.

SUBPLOT AND BACKSTORY

Integral to plot are subplot and backstory. Your book will have both, because every character has a backstory and every narrative has a substory.

I'll leave the advice on backstory to Stephen King, from *On Writing*:

> *The most important things to remember about back story are that (a) everyone has a history and (b) most of it isn't very interesting. Stick to the parts that are, and don't get carried away with the rest. Long life stories are best received in bars, and only then an hour or so before closing time, and if you are buying. (227)*

In other words, don't worry about backstory until you've got a solid forward momentum in your plot, and then start weaving it in digestible bits rather than as an info dump.

As for subplot, typical novels have three or four, and each one must serve a purpose. I like to think of subplots as tiny balances to the main plot as well as ways to humanize your protagonist. If the main story is literary fiction about a newly divorced man making peace with a cancer diagnosis, for example, a subplot could bring in humor, say the cancer patient's young nephew coming to live with him. Or possibly you're writing a horror novel full of terror. A balancing subplot would be a romance between the protagonist and the woman who saves him. Subplots can also show how a character evolves. For example, the friendship that blooms between Dr. Grant and the kids in *Jurassic Park* as they fight off dinosaur attacks shows a growth in the previously commitment- and child-phobic doctor.

Let your subplot flow organically from your primary plot, but make sure not to drop it. The subplot needs to continue until its natural conclusion. Think of your subplot as one strand in a braid, maybe the green thread in a blue friendship bracelet you wove during summer camp. You won't always see the green thread, but it must be consistently running throughout.

In addition, most subplots should be introduced in the first third of the book, usually via a secondary character and involving relationship growth (romance or friendship) in addition to offering a contrasting tone to the central conflict. Sometimes, however, it makes sense to introduce a subplot after a halfway point because of a reversal of fortune.

Got all that? Here's a recap: decide what your character wants more than anything. Introduce that and the characters and the subplots in the first third or so of the book. The rest of the book is about saying no to your protagonist, with all scenes connected and meaningful. At the end of the novel, your protagonist must be a different person than they were at the beginning, and the major loose ends must be tied up. I offer a Mile Marker exercise at the end of the chapter to guide you in laying that out for your own novel.

 In Chapter 5, "Choose Your Novel Concept," you began to think about what you wanted more than anything to help you choose a genre to write in. In Chapter 6, "Craft Compelling Characters," you began to think about your novel's protagonist and what they wanted more than anything. Use what you learned about your character's desires/goals to craft the plot of your novel.

To illustrate how plot lays out in a best-selling novel, in Appendix E, I offer you an overview of the structure of Sandra Cisneros' brilliant, poignant, semi-autobiographical and best-selling *The House on Mango Street*, a book that's standard reading in most high schools. If you're not familiar, *The House on Mango Street* is a coming-of-age story told from the perspective of Esperanza Corben, a twelve-year-old transitioning from girl to woman. What she wants more than anything is the same thing Sandra Cisneros wants more than anything: a house of her own.

I've chosen this story for a plot autopsy for four reasons. The first is that the language and emotion of this book are a love song. I read and reread lines just to feel them against my skin. Second, Cisneros is generous in sharing her inspiration for characters and conflicts in this book. She speaks candidly about them in her memoir, *A House of My Own: Stories from My Life*, in which she writes:

> *This was the period in my life, that slippery age when you're both child and woman and neither, I was to record in* The House on Mango Street. *How was I to know I'd document the women who sat their sadness on an elbow and stared out a window. . . . By the time I finished, my memoir was no longer memoir, no longer autobiographical, and had evolved into a collective story peopled with several lives, from my past and present, placed in one fictional time and neighborhood—* Mango Street. *(81)*

She also speaks about how her life inspired scenes in the book in various interviews, which makes it easier to see how she transformed fact into fiction.

The third reason is that the book itself is an ode to writing's therapeutic power. The character of Esperanza finds her strength and ultimate freedom in writing, as does Cisneros, which makes it a great example for explaining the potential organizational sequence of a healing novel. Finally, *Mango Street* contains a unique structure. It's a series of forty-six vignettes rather than a traditionally woven narrative, which makes it perfect for illustrating how conflict-focused scenes are strung together to create all novels, even ones that don't initially appear to be structured around a cohesive or traditional plot.

The storyline has three main conflicts running through it. Two are internal, and the first is the main plot thread: Esperanza's desire for a home, which is at odds with the family, neighborhood, and on a larger scale, the community she's been born into. The second internal conflict is an often humorous, sometimes terrifying subplot: the push and pull Esperanza experiences between the expectations of childhood and womanhood. The external conflict is sometimes invisible on the page but always present. It falls between a traditional, majority culture literary narrative and the earthy story Cisneros *needed* to tell, a point she foregrounds in *A House of My Own*:

> *It occurred to me that none of the books in this class, in any of my classes, in all the years of my education had ever discussed a house like mine. . . . I wanted to quit school right then and there, but didn't. Instead, I got mad, and anger when it's used to act, when used nonviolently, has power. I asked myself what I could write about that my classmates couldn't. . . . I was trying as best I could to write the kind of book I'd never seen in a library or in a school, the kind of book not even my professors could write. (127–8)*

All the scene conflicts in the novel fall into one of these three categories—the two internal and one external to Cisneros as well as her character Esperanza—and all of them spawn obstacles that are thrown into Esperanza's path as she seeks out what she wants more than anything: a house of her own. Cisneros captured every single beat of the transition from ungrounded to owning a home and from girl to woman in perfect Polaroid snapshots. Every scene is built around a conflict, and every scene is necessary, connected to the one before it and leading to the one after.

Cisneros wrote *The House on Mango Street* over the course of years, across countries and life moments. In the introduction to the twenty-fifth anniversary edition of the book, she writes that in creating the book, she "cut apart and stitched together events to tailor the story, gave it shape so it had a beginning, middle, and end, because real life stories rarely come to us complete. Emotions, though, can't be invented, can't be borrowed. All the emotions my characters feel, good or bad, are mine" (xxii–xxiii). So it must be with your own novel. Each story has its own structure that you have to listen for. If your book is following the "decide what the character wants more than anything and follow them" rule, and one event is directly connected to the next and the stakes are gradually but consistently rising, you're doing fine. Make sure to tie what your protagonist wants more than anything to what *you* want more than anything. This will keep your plot authentic as well as poignant.

Similarly, there is no "set" number of scenes a book requires. *Mango Street* is on the short side, both in page and scene count. A good rule of thumb is around eighty scenes for a book, some short and some longer, and around eighty thousand words for the finished draft. But that's a guideline, not a rule. In the end, your job is to tell your story, the one only you can tell, of the transformation of a character through trials.

The Catalain Book of Secrets, my Kickstarter-funded magical realism novel, is an aces example of this. I drew heavily from the darkest periods of my twenties to write it, and the characters are based on women who are very close to me. The novel explores a family curse that haunts the Catalain women, dimming their magic and exposing them to generational sexual and emotional abuse. You are introduced to the women as they are about to reach the lowest points in their lives. Over the course of the story, through a series of wickedly painful (aren't they all?) transformations, the women begin to reclaim their magic, their power, and their unity as a family. Their transformation through trials is the plot that coheres the entire novel.

In her memoir, Cisneros distills this magic, to her as a writer and us as readers, of crafting a story from life. She writes that creating *The House on Mango Street* "allowed me to speak, to name that thing with a name, that shame of being poor, of being female, of being not quite good enough, and examine where it had come from and why, so I could exchange shame for celebration" (129).

The alchemy of rewriting your life.

Departure. Fulfillment. Return.

 This plotting exercise further refines the novel idea you selected in Chapter 5, "Choose Your Novel Concept," and builds on the characters you were asked to create or expand on in Chapter 6, "Craft Compelling Characters."

PLOT AND SUBPLOT DEVELOPMENT

For this exercise, you're going to decide what you and then what your protagonist wants more than anything, brainstorm obstacles to this goal, and finally, come up with a subplot that complements the main narrative thread.

Step 1

Pull out your notebook. At the top of a new page, write "What I want more than anything is . . . " Set a timer for ten minutes. Write on that prompt constantly, without criticism or correction until the timer goes off.

Step 2

Turn the page. At the top of the new page, write "What my main character wants more than anything is . . . " Reset your timer for ten minutes and freewrite on this new prompt.

Step 3

Turn the page. At the top of the new page, write "The obstacles that are going to keep my main character from reaching this goal are . . . " Reset your timer for ten minutes and freewrite on this third prompt.

Step 4

Review what you wrote for Steps 1, 2, and 3, underlining anything that resonates. Transcribe the most powerful concept you just underlined into the center of a new journal page. Do this for each concept you underlined, giving each its own new page. Once you're done, return to the first concept you gave its own page and mind-map it, that is, jot down any words or phrases that pop into your head when you think of that concept, sprouting them out like octopus arms. Your goal is to explore and refine the concepts. Mind-map each of your concept pages in this fashion. See the following visual example if mind mapping is new to you.

Step 5

When you are finished mind mapping your concepts, at the top of the new page, write "Things that are important to my main character but aren't the character's main goal are . . . " Set a timer for ten minutes. Write in response to this final prompt constantly, without criticism or correction until the timer goes off.

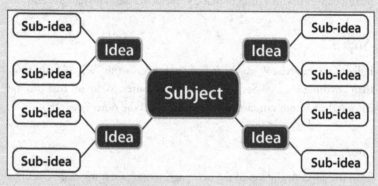

Example of a Mind Map

CHAPTER 8

CREATE A SENSE OF PLACE

Words can be like X-rays if you use them properly—they'll go through anything. You read and you're pierced.
—*Aldous Huxley*

The sense of place is as essential to good and honest writing as a logical mind; surely they are somewhere related. It is by knowing where you stand that you grow able to judge where you are.
—*Eudora Welty*

Nobel Prize–winning Alice Munro set her *Lives of Girls and Women* in her native Huron County, Ontario. Stephen King's *The Shining* is set in the Colorado Rockies'-based Overlook Hotel, a fictional location inspired by a night he and his wife, Tabitha, spent as the only guests of the Stanley Hotel in Estes Park, Colorado. Both Beverly Cleary and her beloved Ramona Quimby grew up near Klickitat Street in Portland, Oregon. J. D. Salinger, born and raised in Manhattan, drops Holden Caulfield into the same setting in *Catcher in the Rye*.

There's impressive precedent for placing your novel in a location you're familiar with. Writers call on their personal experience to create vivid settings far more than they call on life experiences to create plot and even more so than they weave characters out of the people in their lives.

You should definitely mine your memories to build a cinematic setting.

I'm going to tell you how, but first, I want to make sure we're on the same page about setting and why it's important, because in my experience, most people have a one-dimensional idea of setting. For example, if I asked you where the musical *Chicago* is set, you'd tell me *Chicago*, and you wouldn't be wrong.

You wouldn't entirely be right, either.

Let me demonstrate.

Here, using ten words, I describe where I grew up:

Claw bangs   *stolen sweet wine summers*
turkey farms   *snowy winters*

If I'd simply told you I grew up in central Minnesota, you'd recognize the location but not really get the *setting*. I could even add a time frame, make it "central Minnesota in the '80s," and you'd have a better idea of the terrain that produced me, but you wouldn't have anything substantial to hold onto, and for setting to work, it must engage the readers' senses and evoke a clear image.

Try it yourself. First, name the city or region where you grew up.

OK, now write the era.

Finally, in ten or fewer words, *show* rather than *tell* me the setting.

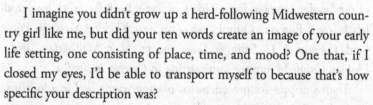

I imagine you didn't grow up a herd-following Midwestern country girl like me, but did your ten words create an image of your early life setting, one consisting of place, time, and mood? One that, if I closed my eyes, I'd be able to transport myself to because that's how specific your description was?

Excellent.

You need to do that in your writing, always. Setting in a narrative is not simply a place or a time. Cinematic setting in fiction is an interplay of both, plus mood, presented through facts (names of places, dates, etc.) as well as sensory (sight, sound, smell, taste, and touch) detail, which in turn interact to affect both writer and reader and, often, plot and character.

HOW SETTING AFFECTS YOU AS A WRITER

If I told you to imagine a hospital's smell, I bet you could call it up immediately: antiseptic, sharp, and depending on your personal experience, terrifying or comforting. Smell is the most evocative of the senses. Scientists believe the reason is that our olfactory bulb is right next to the amygdala and hippocampus, the parts of our brain that process memories and emotion. Vision, touch, and sound do not pass through the same area and so, scientists hypothesize, are not as connected in our memories.

Evoking smell is a great tool for writers. In fact, the phenomena of smell calling up vivid memories is referred to as the Proust Phenomenon after the scene in Proust's *In Search of Lost Time* where the character smells and tastes a madeleine cookie and is transported to his childhood. If you know the importance of sensory detail to creating vivid setting, and how effective it is in engaging your readers and connecting them to your story, then you'll wield setting like it's your job.

However, this Proust Phenomenon can also be uncomfortable verging on distressing, as many of the same setting tools used to evoke emotions in your readers will also evoke emotions and potentially memories in you. Again, smell is the worst offender, particularly for those suffering from PTSD. A scent that most would find unpleasant, say the smell of diesel fuel, might trigger a vivid wartime memory for a veteran, for example.

It isn't just smell, though, that can be a powerful connector. Mentally revisiting a location to write about it may activate a suppressed memory of something that happened at that location. The memory could be positive, but research finds that emotionally-charged experiences are more likely to be spontaneously remembered than non-emotional experiences.

For example, I have a friend who is a college speech teacher. She told me the story of a student who was so nervous for her first speech that she came to class in a full-length winter jacket. As it was February in Minnesota, this behavior wasn't odd. The problem came when the student removed her jacket and looked down to see she'd been so scared of public speaking that she'd forgotten to wear pants. I bet for the rest of her life, if she's ever in a room that smells like that classroom, she's plunged right into that mortifying memory. We all have our own versions of humiliation, shame, trauma, joy—any primal emotion—that we can and should call on to craft a vibrant setting, but tread cautiously in this area more than any other.

Rewriting your life lets you process your past so it can't sneak up on you.

This process is powerful, but it can also be painful, so I'm going to clarify that rewriting your life isn't a replacement for professional help. I was seeing a therapist every other week the year after Jay died, and I was sharing my experiences and fears with friends and family. To this day, I visit a good therapist every few months for a tune-up, more frequently if I need it. Living a healthy life is a marathon, not a sprint, and rewriting your life is a piece to the puzzle rather than a magic bullet.

 Chapter 1, "The Science of Writing to Heal," overviewed how writing therapy helps people to heal from past trauma. Writing about an emotionally impactful experience through the safety of fiction switches out one of three steps in the stimulus-significance-response pattern, allowing you more control in how you perceive and respond to memories as well as current situations.

If properly wielded, however, intentionally calling on past experiences to write compelling fiction allows you to gently access your crucible moments so that you can heal from them and use them in service of your story.

HOW TO CREATE EPIC FICTIONAL SETTINGS

Vivid settings are foundational to compelling fiction. While settings tied to locations where you experienced something sad or traumatic or exceptional often pack an extra punch, it's not a requirement that you call on painful memories to write a fantastic setting. The settings just have to be richly portrayed, which, unless you have a secret superpower in this area, is easier to do if you've visited the places you're writing about.

As an example of how setting your novel in a familiar location allows you to bring added depth to your tale, check out this excerpt from Khaled Hosseini's moving *A Thousand Splendid Suns*, a novel that is in many ways an homage to his birthplace of Kabul, Afghanistan. He gracefully weaves time, place, and mood to create setting:

In the summer of 2000, the drought reached its third and worst year.

In Helmand, Zabol, Kandahar, villages turned into herds of nomadic communities, always moving, searching for water and green pastures for their livestock. When they found neither, when their goats and sheep and cows died off, they came to Kabul. They took to the Kareh-Ariana hillside, living in makeshift slums, packed in huts, fifteen or twenty at a time. That was also the summer of Titanic . . .

People smuggled pirated copies of the film from Pakistan—sometimes in their underwear. After curfew, everyone locked their doors, turned out the lights, turned down the volume, and reaped tears for Jack and Rose and the passengers of the doomed ship. (269)

In the preceding, notice how setting must be multidimensional. Effective setting takes place at the intersection of place (Kabul), time (summer of 2000), and mood (the black humor of people suffering from a drought obsessing over *Titanic*). Remove any one of those three legs, and the table falls flat.

Let me elaborate on how place, time, and mood intersect in well-written fiction.

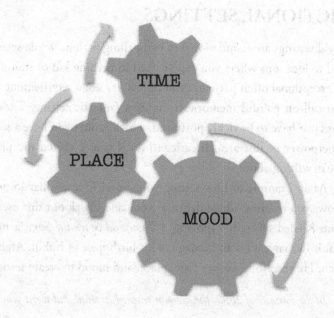

Location

Location is the most obvious component of setting. Laura Ingalls Wilder's autobiographical novel *On the Banks of Plum Creek* would have been a very different book if not set in Walnut Grove, Minnesota. Malcolm Lowry's *Under the Volcano*, which was ranked eleventh in Modern Library's 100 Best Novels list, was set in a fictionalized Cuernavaca, Mexico, where Lowry was living as he wrote. The story needed to be set in Mexico to capitalize on the character-building or -destroying effects of being a stranger in a strange land. Without it, it would have simply been another story of a drunk Brit.

When you're thinking about the primary location for your story, remember that it's not simply about an address. All three of the legs of setting—location, time, and mood—have two dimensions: your writing goal and how you want to achieve it. Think back to the beginning of the chapter and my description of where I grew up. My goal (the "where") was to place you smack dab in central Minnesota, but central Minnesota is a different place for different people. I wanted to describe *my* central Minnesota, which I achieved (the "how") by listing the defining characteristics that make me both love and despise my old stomping grounds. Here is more detail of how to choose the where and how of the location portion of your setting.

Where

You might already know in what geographical place your novel will be set. The location may have sprung organically from the characters you want to bring in or the plot you want to follow, or maybe you started with a place and selected your concept backward from there. If, however, you haven't yet decided where you'll set your novel, I recommend choosing either where you live now or a location with strong resonance for you, as the story allows. You will be in fine company.

How

The next step is to decide how to convey that place with intimacy and poignancy. This sentence from Alice Munro's *Lives of Girls and Women* demonstrates the where (Jubilee) and the how of conveying Jubilee ("dull, simple, amazing, and unfathomable"):

> *People's lives, in Jubilee as elsewhere, were dull, simple, amazing, and unfathomable—deep caves paved with kitchen linoleum. (253)*

To recap, it's not enough to simply state the location of your story. Whenever you mention place, make sure you include not only the where but the how.

Let me give one more example of the interplay of where and how. I wrote the first book in my young adult *Toadhouse Trilogy* because I wanted to write something my kids could read, and my semi-raunchy mysteries weren't cutting it. Plus, I wanted to capture a certain period in their lives. So, the original idea for that series sprang from the characters. Once I had chosen them, an older sister named Aine (an Irish name pronounced "Aw-knee") who both resents and loves her little brother, Spenser, I decided to go meta and write a book about books. Specifically, I chose the concept that characters can actually travel inside of novels—*A Tale of Two Cities, The Ramayana, The Adventures of Tom Sawyer*, and so on.

I started with character, and that inspired plot.

I had only to choose setting.

Because I wanted the book to open with the children unknowingly residing inside a famous novel, I set them in *The Adventures of Tom Sawyer*, which dictated that my book open in Missouri. I've only barely passed through the Show Me state but for various reasons I wanted to set my novel there (one, really: I didn't want to get sued for setting my story in someone else's novel and so needed to choose one that was both famous and in the public domain; hence, *Tom Sawyer*), and so I began doing exactly what you should do if you need to set your novel somewhere you've never been: I started researching. I went online to learn about the weather, the geography, what plants grow there, and especially what the area I wanted to write about looked like. Google Earth is amazing for this, and free, as long as you have Internet access.

But all of that research just gave me the first dimension of location—the where. I still didn't know how to convey it. For that, I called on two pivotal childhood memories, one positive and one negative. The positive memory is of my sister and me playing hide-and-go-seek in the woods. We got so good at it that we'd blindfold ourselves (with sheets—never go small when you can go big) and hunt each other like clumsy animals. In this recollection, everything is dusted with a childhood, Alice-in-Wonderland sense of awe over the simple magic of being alive in a world where worms can dig, birds can fly, and enormous trees sprout from a tiny seed. The second memory is my recurring childhood nightmare of being terrorized on a riverbank.

Combining the what—Missouri and all its facts—with the how—the thrill and terror of being alone in the woods and by the river—resulted in this setting:

Her heart thudding, she curls herself small, like a chipmunk. The tight space reeks of mushrooms and a basement she can't remember. Through force of will and much practice, she steadies her breathing. That or her smell will surely give her away. Using tiny movements, she cradles moss over her raw elbow to mask the iron odor of the fresh wound. In this hunt, out of sight most definitely does not equal out of mind.

Overhead, a northern mockingbird trills, its song a repeated *weep weep, weep weep*.

Footsteps sound nearby almost immediately, surprisingly quiet.

Swish, swish.

She'd found cover in the nick of time. Outside her sycamore, the grass parts. Two sharp intakes seek her scent. Her heartbeat picks up, racing with the rat-a-tat of a woodpecker. She swallows her breath and melts deeper into the cave of the tree, becoming bark and branch.

It works. He steps past the gnarly sycamore with its girl heart.

Her clenched fists loosen.

She waits a handful of beats before poking her head out. No sign of him, just dense hardwoods forming a canopy so thick only ferns and horsebalm sprout beneath it, plus the occasional patch of grass where sunbeams are fighting their way through. The dappled light gives the forest an underwater quality, making it both vibrant and hazy. It smells humid, almost tropical. She must reach the river.

If you think something terrifying happens on the riverbank, just as it did in my recurring nightmares, you're right. And, for the record, that nightmare hasn't returned since I wrote about it. This is one of the gorgeous fruits of this process of rewriting your life—you get to process and release what no longer serves you.

As a side note, if you choose to write about an actual geographical location, know that there are two camps on this topic. One says don't set your novel in a real location because best case, you cheese off people because you didn't get it perfect, and worst case, you get sued. The other tells you to write the real so people can feel that connection, either because they can or they have visited the place. As someone who has done both, I'm not sure which camp I'd pitch a tent in, though if I am writing about something bad happening, I *always* make the place fictional. So, while my humorous mystery series is set in the real town of Battle Lake, Minnesota, where I lived for a number of years, all the murders happen in fictional businesses or houses. While I am not a lawyer and so have no legal advice to offer, my suggestion is that you protect yourself, always, and when in doubt as to whether or not to use a real place, err on the side of caution.

Another aside: if you want to work in social issues without being didactic, using place is a good way to do it. For example, if water issues are important to you, you could set the story in modern times near Lake Superior or Las Vegas or some location where the politics of water would naturally arise.

Time

Like location, time has two dimensions in your fiction: the when and the how. The when is self-evident. The how, unless you're writing a story set in exactly your world and the time that you're writing in, requires research. Because *The Toadhouse Trilogy* opens in late 1800s Missouri, I needed to research the specifics of language, clothes, technology, and the customs of that period to convey the time. Here's an example:

> After she and Spenser are inside, she locks the door that's never been locked, pulls the curtains tight over the windows, then distracts herself by bustling over to the cupboards.
>
> "Cheese dreams okay for lunch?"
>
> It's Spenser's favorite meal. He nods happily.
>
> Aine slices four slabs of homemade bread and next unwraps the papered white cheese that Mondegreen buys in town. She cuts two slices and arranges them on the bread before slapping a generous pat of butter into the cast iron pan and holding a lit match over the gas burner.

Grilled cheese sandwiches were referred to as "cheese dreams" in the late 1800s, bread was homemade, cheese came wrapped in paper, and if you were lucky enough to have a stove that was not powered by wood, it was powered by gas or kerosene. All of those details are the "how" of the time period I chose.

It really is the small, specific details that capture time. If you are writing true historical fiction, note also that your readers will be sticklers for accuracy. Make sure to get it all right. If you're visual like me, I encourage you to tag or print out photos of time and place so that you can provide accurate descriptions. The New York Public Library has gone a long way toward helping writers obtain visual inspiration by putting nearly two hundred thousand (as of this writing) maps, photographs, postcards, and other amazing research into the public domain. You can access this resource by going online and searching for the library database.

Mood

Place is the where of your story; time, the when; and mood, the what. For my money, the mood is the most interesting leg in setting's three-legged structure. Ominous, funny, nail-biting, ironic, caustic, loving. Unless you're writing noir, gothic romance, or horror, your story's mood will change with the scene rather than be fixed to the story. Mood is a crucial component of a well-crafted narrative, and it calls upon all five senses.

In writing a scene for *Toadhouse* where I wanted to evoke terror, for example, I used sound, taste, touch, sight, and smell:

The knock, when it comes, echoes like a guillotine.

Rap rap rap. Rap rap rap.

A matched knocking, only louder, echoes through Aine's ribcage. Terror tastes like burnt chalk on her tongue. In the five years since they'd come to live in Grandma Glori's house on the edge of the woods, only two people besides Mondegreen have ever visited. Both times, before answering the door, Glori had warned them. *Hear that sound? You don't ever answer it. For anyone.*

No one has knocked other than those two times. Until now.

"Shush," Aine whispers, unnecessarily.

Spenser is as white as bone. He's gripping the edge of the table. In a burst of insight, Aine realizes he has their mom's long, elegant fingers, the beautiful hands of a piano player. She hurries over and hugs him, her heart pumping in her skull.

"Quick, back here." Aine pushes Spenser to a more protected spot behind the woodstove. He doesn't know the size of the space he is being shoved into, so she has to tuck his arms and legs in for him. His knee scrapes along a sharp corner, drawing blood.

"Will he be able to see me?" Spenser's voice is small and painfully frightened, the paper-thin sound of new ice cracking.

It breaks her heart to peel his hands off of her, but she has to.

Although calling on all five senses is important when you want to craft a particularly vibrant and memorable scene, don't go overboard. Setting should be authentic without being intrusive. If it slows down the forward momentum of the story or is thrown in simply for the sake of writing a setting, don't use it.

Another point to remember is that if quick movements are part of the time, place, or mood you're conveying, know your layout. Don't write an island in the center of the kitchen in one scene and have it be an open layout kitchen in the next. I recommend sketching floor plans for consistency, which the Map exercise at the end of this chapter will guide you in doing.

Ultimately, I hope you'll find creating setting an organic by-product of your writing and a chance to travel on a budget. I mean that seriously. When I succeed in building a truly cinematic setting, one that weaves place, time, and mood through a perfect balance of facts and sensory detail, I am living within the narrative as I write, smelling Chinatown as my character flees an assassin, tasting the glorious soup she slurps up after a day of hard labor, hearing the impossibly fragile music of flutes as she steals a kiss in the back of the orchestra room.

SETTING CIRCLE

For this exercise, you're going to make (1) a setting circle and (2) a setting sketch for a potential scene in your novel. Your goal is to practice wielding both components of all three legs of effective setting and doing it invisibly so as not to pull your reader out of the story.

Here's what you do: think of a pivotal scene in the novel you're going to write, possibly the one that sets the whole story in motion. For my young adult book, the inciting incident happens on the porch of the grandmother's house, where she's struck down and the children are forced to flee. Sketch the layout for your own inciting scene. Then, fill out a setting circle for it. A setting circle is a handy-dandy visual organizer that allows you to brainstorm the time (when and how you will convey it), place (where and how you'll convey it), and mood (what and how you'll convey it) of a setting. I've used an example from *The Toadhouse Trilogy* to demonstrate how sketching the layout of and crafting a setting wheel for a pivotal scene could look.

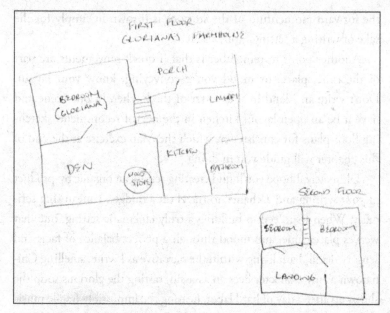

Layout Sketch of My Scene

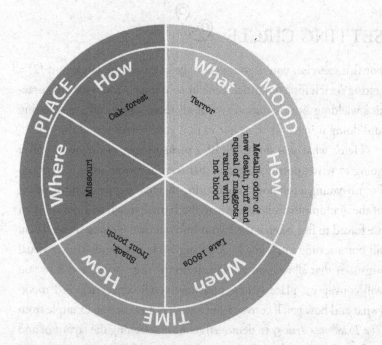

Setting Circle for My Scene

Here's the scene that resulted from that layout sketch and setting circle.

The blue weapons crawl off of him like worms and fly toward Glori. She drops the marble and curves her right hand into a claw. She clutches at her chest as if removing her heart and flings her hand at the woods. A roar of pain flies back.

"You can't help her," Gilgamesh says, surprisingly close. "I will carry you if you don't move. Do not let her sacrifice be for nothing."

But Aine cannot look away. Her mouth is still open in a soundless cry.

The blue maggots squirm toward the shack and her grandma. Then a strange thing happens. The salt ring stops them. They puff and squeal when they approach it.

Glori ignores them and sketches shapes in the air. The forms resemble Mondegreen's, intersecting lines and twisting ivy, except hers are a rainbow of colors and twice as large.

The breeze begins to hum. Glori keeps her eyes pinned on the forest, beyond Mondegreen's still form, attention absolutely focused. The trees begin to part. The roar in the woods has become primal and huge. The air around Glori is so thick with the shadows of shapes that it pulses.

Whatever has killed Mondegreen is about to emerge into the clearing.

Aine's legs move instinctively and she races toward her grandma. Despite her soul-deep terror, despite the certainty that if she follows Gilgamesh, she will be reunited with her mother, she can't leave Glori to fight that horrible, unseen creature by herself.

A bellow of pure hate echoes out of the forest.

Glori's eyes widen and the blood seeps from her face. She is staring straight south, into the oak forest. She has just laid eyes on the monster moving toward her. Glori turns to Aine, and Aine sees it clearly on her grandmother's face: surprise mixed with resignation. But no fear.

Later, she will remember being surprised there was no fear.

"I'm coming!" Aine yells.

A proud smile flashes across Glori's face for an instant before it is replaced with a look of supreme concentration.

But time has run out.

The blue force in the forest has arched and focused until with a crack, it's shaped itself into an arrow that sears toward Glori. The air crackles and reeks of fresh lightning. The acid blue bolt screams directly toward her grandmother. Glori has time to snatch only one shape out of the air, only one final chance to save her own life.

"Scaoiligí!" She hurls the word at Spenser and Aine.

It hits Aine like a wall.

She drops to her knees.

The sensation is good, powerful, prickly. She smells a blast of cinnamon and allspice then breathes in air purely for the first time in five years. The vibrancy of freshness and green overpowers her senses. She raises her eyes to Grandma Glori and they lock stares. Aine is aware of a deep connection that lasts only for a moment.

It feels like love.

In that instant, scissoring blue blades hurtle through the air, flying directly over the spot where the salt lines did not meet because Jake had slashed the bag.

The rogue blades slice Glori in two.

Aine's legs go out from under her. She can't trust her eyes.

The mutilation happens so quickly that Glori's hand, still stretched into a claw, is hovering in the air for a moment after her top is separated from her bottom.

The giant marble falls to the ground first.

It's rained with hot blood.

Time stands still for a moment that lasts forever. Then the two halves of Glori's body drop to the porch with a terrible thud. The air is saturated with the metallic odor of new death.

Aine's eyes cloud and she is unable to breathe.

The suddenness, the permanence. She is stunned beyond reaction.

Grandma Glori has been murdered.

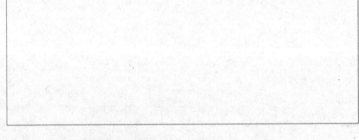

Sketch Your Scene Layout

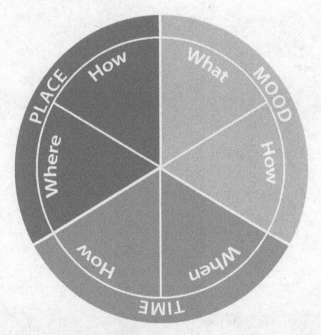

Your Scene's Setting Circle

CHAPTER 9

PULL IT ALL TOGETHER

A book should serve as an axe for the frozen sea within us.
                                        —*Franz Kafka*

I like shape very much. A novel has to have shape, and life doesn't have any.

                                        —*Jean Rhys*

In Chapter 4, you explored which genre you would write in. Chapter 5 guided you to select your concept, Chapter 6 to turn bits of people from your life into compelling fictional characters, Chapter 7 to distill life into plot, and Chapter 8 to select and transform places you've been or locations you've researched into cinematic settings. Now it's time to connect all those pieces and build your novel. This step is normally scary, but if you've been completing the writing exercises in each chapter, you have everything you need to soar.

I wasn't so lucky when I started my first book or my second or even my third. If I'm honest with myself (and you), it's not exactly ancient history that the idea of drafting a novel felt like being dropped into central Africa's Congo Basin with a compass and a paperclip.

Naked.

Rolled in honey.

With everyone I've ever wanted to impress watching via a live feed, gathered together in a room, eating popcorn and laughing so hard that they spewed schadenfreude all over the television.

When I began drafting *May Day*, I spent much of my writing time feeling overwhelmed at the scope of what I'd taken on and like a ridiculous fraud for even pretending I could write a book. I grew up in rural Minnesota, for crying in the night. Not only did I not know any writers, I hardly knew anyone who liked to *read*.

But there was personal treasure to be mined in the writing of a novel; I sensed it even then, rubies of resilience and emeralds of hope, and so I read what I could on the craft of writing, sought out mentors, and read fiction like a chef trying to puzzle out the recipe by tasting the meal. After five years of trial and error, I finally arrived at a method to reduce the time and stress of crafting an experience-based novel while increasing the joy of writing and the quality of the story.

I call this technique the Pyramid on Point (POP) method because it balances the entire novel-writing process around the tip, or the point, of your idea. All writers end up with a unifying theme across the books that they write and that theme is the most indigestible nugget in their mental compost pile.

For example, I write about the poison and power of secrets. In. Every. Single. Book. While it took writing eight novels to realize it, I come by this meta-theme honestly. I grew up in a house built on fear and secrets, liberally sprinkled with alcoholism, psychedelic drugs, swingers, and naked volleyball parties. I saw enough dangling wieners and bouncing boobs in the '70s to last a lifetime. I packed my first bong before I was ten and mixed a mean whiskey water by age twelve. To this day, I think my mom and dad's worst fear was that I'd rebel and turn Republican. My parents will be mortified to discover I am writing about them or my childhood. This, along with an instilled allegiance to secrets, has kept me from writing nonfiction up until this moment. How am I finally breaking free of this, you ask? The advice to write as if your parents are dead seems too harsh. I'm instead electing to write as if they're illiterate.

My experience of sifting through my mental compost pile via novel writing is not unique. At a recent writing conference, a famous dominatrix and successful noir author confessed to me that all her books are about that pivotal, cathartic moment when a person tests their limits. Many of John Irving's novels contain a recurring theme of younger men who are seduced or abused by older women. Parental abandonment appears in every one of Charles Dickens' books. Amy Tan tackles mother-daughter relationships in her stories. You will find some version of your own experience-based theme in all the novels you write.

 As covered in Chapter 5, "Choose Your Novel Concept," you'll find that most if not all your ideas are already hiding, ready to be plucked, in the compost pile of your mind. Remember that your compost pile is that fertile, loamy, shit-filled place where you tossed your baggage in the hopes that it would decompose on its own. It doesn't. You have to stir it up and spread it out. It's just the way it works.

Don't worry if you don't know your life theme right now; discovering it is one of the many gifts of novel writing. What I need you to do now is take your hottest idea and work it through the POP method that follows. This method leads you through seven manageable steps that transform your life experiences into a novel, regardless of how much writing experience you've had. Because of the work you've begun in the previous chapters, you already have a good base for your characters, plot, and setting. Now it's time to pull it all together and write that book. Grab your journal and pen, because here we go.

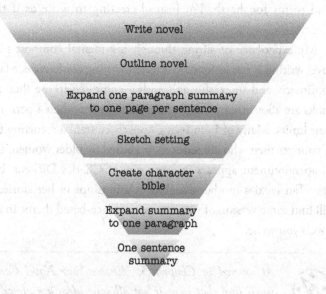

Write novel

Outline novel

Expand one paragraph summary to one page per sentence

Sketch setting

Create character bible

Expand summary to one paragraph

One sentence summary

STEP 1: FIRST, SUMMARIZE YOUR NOVEL IN ONE SENTENCE

Open a new page in your journal. If you didn't already do this in Chapter 5, distill the overarching concept of the novel you will write into its purest form: a single sentence. Don't include specific names or places now; the idea is to be purely conceptual.

I'll use a work by one of my favorite authors, Isabel Allende, as an example. Allende is no stranger to converting her pleasure and pain into best-selling novels. As I wrote earlier, *The House of the Spirits*, her first book, entered this world as a letter she was writing to her dying grandfather.

At the time, Allende was in exile from her home country, unable to visit her grandfather, and struggling with deep grief. In a *Washington*

Post interview on the writing of *The House of the Spirits*, she said, "I had lost everything I had. It was a crazy attempt to recover everything . . . in those pages." She instinctually drew on and fictionalized her rawest pain, cloaking her specific experiences in imagination and weaving them together to craft a lush, evocative novel that became an international bestseller, award-winning movie, and popular play. Here is what Step 1 of the POP method would look like for *The House of the Spirits*:

> *Standing in for Chile, patriarch Esteban Trueba grows from child to elder, struggling against and then embracing the revolutionary flow of life.*

Notice how that sentence is neat and sweet? It's tempting to pack lots of detail into your one-sentence summary. Your idea is complex, your characters multifaceted, your setting diverse. How can you condense all of that to a handful of words? Remember my Chapter 5 example, my brain-dump crack at what *Eve*, the magical realism novel that I'm writing simultaneous to this book, will be about?

> The year is 1907, and seventeen-year-old Eve Catalain has arrived to Faith Falls, Minnesota, along with the quarter-century rising of the snakes. As beautiful and elusive as a firefly, she has captured the eye of Crucifer Darkly and Ennis Patterson equally. Crucifer is wicked and wealthy, the source of dark rumors, respected to his face and feared behind his back. Ennis is twenty years older than Eve, quiet, kind, and wretchedly content to be her friend. When Eve defies Crucifer's command to never enter his mansion at night, she uncovers a secret the town would kill to keep hidden. How she responds will either cement her personal power or curse generations of Catalain women to come.

Besides being far too long, this summary includes extraneous detail that is important to me but not crucial to the task. Again, the goal is to take an aerial snapshot of your novel, capturing only the large structure. If you search online for "*New York Times* bestseller list," you'll find an excellent example of this type of concise description accompanying each book on the list. Trim your initial vision so your sentence is as succinct as those descriptions. After I cut away the subplots, supporting characters, and superficial detail, I am left with this one-sentence summary of *Eve*:

> Seventeen-year-old Eve Catalain must learn to trust in her own power when she uncovers the terrible secret binding the people of the not-quite-right town of pre–WWI Faith Falls, Minnesota.

If you craft this sentence with accuracy and poignancy, it will feed you during the lean times of self-doubt, be your northern light in the writing process, and, if you are so inclined, give you a snappy line to share with friends and family who ask what you're working on. Once you're satisfied with your sentence, it's time to move on to Step 2.

STEP 2: EXPAND YOUR SINGLE SENTENCE INTO A ONE-PARAGRAPH-SUMMARY

Step 2 is a summary of your entire novel and should be written in your journal immediately below your Step 1 sentence. Summarize the status quo at the opening of your novel, what obstacles the protagonist encounters, and how the novel ends. This isn't the time for secrets. Lay it all out.

Refer to the writing exercises you completed in Chapter 7 for this step. If it is helpful, freewrite or mind-map even further, using key names or phrases from your Step 1 sentence as your launch point. Based on my one-sentence overview of *The House of the Spirits*, for example, I would write "Chile," "Esteban Trueba," and/or "revolutionary flow of life" onto the top of a clean sheet of paper and freewrite for ten minutes, penning anything that came to mind without pausing to criticize or proofread. As you know, you'll be amazed at the insight you can access through freewriting.

Once you have a solid idea of the major plot points of your novel as a result of what you read in Chapter 7, freewriting, mind-mapping, or any other tool that works for you, write your full paragraph summary. Here is that Step 1 single-sentence summary of *The House of the Spirits* expanded into a full paragraph (spoiler alert in case this book, or the Meryl Streep film that came after it, is new to you):

> The book opens with sisters Clara and Rosa del Valle living in a fictionalized Chile. Clara, an avid diary-keeper, is able to see the future. When Rosa is accidentally poisoned, Clara takes her place as Esteban Trueba's wife. In the interim, Esteban had gone from a poor miner to a wealthy but often cruel rancher. The first woman he rapes, Pancha, becomes pregnant with his son. His wife, Clara, bears three children. The oldest, Bianca, falls in love with Esteban's foreman's son, and the second third of the story is devoted to their forbidden romance. When Bianca becomes pregnant out of wed-lock, Esteban whips Bianca, strikes Clara, forces Bianca to marry another man, and cuts three fingers off the father of her child. The final third of the story is devoted to Alba, the illegitimate child of that relationship and the only one who still speaks with Esteban. Alba falls in love with a revolutionary named Miguel, who was present at her birth but whom she hasn't seen since. The grand-son of the first woman Esteban raped is now a military leader, who kidnaps, tortures, and rapes Alba, bringing the cycle started by Esteban to a close. Esteban helps Bianca and the foreman's son, both of them now middle-aged, to escape prison, frees Alba, and dies in Alba's arms with Clara's spirit as a witness. The book ends with Alba promising forgiveness and writing the book that becomes The House of the Spirits.

Breathtaking, right? And because of the seamless paper wall that fiction provides its writers, we don't know which of the above story threads are plucked whole from Allende's personal struggles and which are purely products of her imagination. Ultimately, not only is it not any of our business, it also doesn't matter. The only thing that counts is that Allende drew directly from her well of challenging life experiences to craft a complex novel. Writing from her truth healed Allende, as she states in a 1989 interview with William Zissner:

> *In the process of writing the anecdotes of the past, and recalling emotions and pains of my fate, and telling part of the history of my country, I found life became more comprehensible and the world more tolerable. I felt that my roots had been recovered and that during that patient exercise of daily writing I had also recovered my own soul. (44)*

A bonus? Her authenticity, earnestness, and vulnerability made this book an international bestseller.

Of course, Isabel Allende didn't use the POP method when she wrote *The House of the Spirits*, and she certainly didn't have that summary of her own book. She simply typed for a year until she wrote five hundred pages that looked an awful lot like a novel. You can select that route, too, but I find that structure makes the novel-writing process less daunting. For that reason, I suggest that before you draft your book, you come up with a one-sentence summary (Step 1) and expand that sentence into a full paragraph that touches on the main plot points of the book (Step 2) like I did for *The House of the Spirits*.

Note that you must give away the ending to make this Step 2 paragraph work. This summary is for your eyes only, and it's dynamic. You'll find yourself returning to tweak it as you continue, and that's okay. You're writing a book, not a contract. Revising as new ideas occur is one of the exciting elements of writing.

Now comes my personal favorite step.

STEP 3: INVITE YOUR CHARACTERS IN

Now is the time to expand your sourcebook, or character bible, profiling each of your significant characters.

I usually handwrite my character bibles in journals I now create for each novel, but a computer works just as well. If you use writing software like Scrivener, you'll find premade character templates at your fingertips. Devote at least a page to each character, drawing from the cast that began to populate your budding story as soon as you nailed down your concept in Chapter 5 and that you expanded on as you explored your characters in Chapter 6. Include the following information if you haven't already:

- *Name and photograph.* The photo is optional, but if you come across a picture of someone in a magazine or newspaper or an old family photograph that reminds you of your character, slipping that photo into the character's page works wonders to spur creativity and flesh out characterization. For example, I intend to include a photo of Kathy Bates as *Misery*'s Annie Wilkes in my character bible for *Eve.* Her psycho nurse looks very much like Aunt Bea, the babysitter who locked my sister and me in the closet and let her son perform terrifying puppet shows for us, and I'm going to include her as a character in flashbacks to her early life to flesh her out and build sympathy for her.

- *Physical characteristics.* This includes the basics of height, weight, hair and eye color, and so on. This information is particularly useful for characters who won't appear a lot or who will show up across a series. Because you've compiled these details, when these characters do pop up, you'll know just where to look for a physical description of them. Remember to think physically quirky, too.

- *Age.* Include the actual birth date if it's relevant.

- *Personality traits and their source.* For example, is a character lazy because their mother always picked up after them? Do they love baseball because it's the only game their father ever played with them? Do they try to control every person in their life because their childhood lacked stability?[1] Are they steadfast, honest, outgoing, introverted, a space cadet, moody, and if so, why?

- *Quirks and coping mechanisms.* These are one or two imperfections that make your character human, such as a tendency to hum when nervous or a snaggletooth that makes them reluctant to smile.

- *Goals and motivation.* Ask yourself what your character wants and why they want it. Put your own heart and secrets in here, as outlined in Chapter 6.

- *Conflict.* List the obstacles, large and small, that the characters face in achieving their goals.

- *Growth.* This is also called the character arc. How is this character going to be different at the end of this novel? Is their worldview changed? Their heart opened? Think about how you would like to change as you brainstorm this section, because as your protagonist grows, so grow you.

Remember that as their creator, you always need to know more about your characters than your reader ever sees. This inside information allows you to create a multidimensional, internally consistent population for your novel, but you're not going to dump it all into the novel any more than you'd share every detail of your own life with someone you just met.

---

[1] Just spitballing with this one.

Be aware that the character bible is an easy place to get side-tracked; keep your character outlines to one or two pages per person so the process doesn't morph from novel writing to scrapbooking. Also know that this step may be an emotional trigger because you will be digging deep into human motivation as well as the consequences of human choice. Take breaks when you need to and remember that you control the pace, rate, and direction of everything that happens to the characters in your story.

STEP 4: SKETCH YOUR SETTINGS

Building on what you learned and practiced in Chapter 8, draw the street layout and the interior space(s) where most of your story will take place. You will likely have several sketches.

 You will find that, like your characters, your setting naturally follows the life challenge you chose as your novel-worthy concept in Chapter 5, "Choose Your Novel Concept."

No fear when you get to this step; you don't need to be an artist to handle it. If you're sketching a room, for example, just chicken-scratch the major pieces of furniture and placement of windows and doors, as well as which direction is north. If your book is set mostly in a neighborhood or town, sketch out the relevant cross streets and scribble labeled boxes where you imagine all the businesses and houses would be. Obtain an actual city map if you are setting your novel in a real location so you can reference street names and landmarks.

The setting sketches anchor your writing and create consistency and plausibility. Also, they are crucial to writing cinematic action scenes, whether your character is being chased through the alleyways of New York's Meatpacking District or throwing punches in a living room as the furniture splinters. If you have space, staple in a photo or two if you come across an image that captures an element of your setting, and use Google Earth and other online research to fill in any details your memory cannot.

STEP 5: DEVELOP EACH SENTENCE IN STEP 2 INTO A FULL-PAGE DESCRIPTION

Include at least two sound, two smell, and two touch details on each page. For example, let's take the first sentence of *The House of the Spirits* summary that I created in Step 2:

> The book opens with sisters Clara and Rosa del Valle living in a fictionalized Chile.

If I were to expand this to one page, I would describe the characters' features, the smell and flavor of the country, the feel of wind or sun against their skin, the clank and clamor of the countryside. I would include preliminary research into the political issues, mores, and technological breakthroughs of Chile during that period so I could insert accurate conversational topics and make sure I got the clothes and hairstyles just right. I'd brainstorm and roughly outline the give-and-take that would occur if two sisters were talking about a man one of them was going to marry. Use your journal to explore and develop every sentence of your own summary in this way.

STEP 6: COMPLETE A *ROUGH* OUTLINE OF THE NOVEL

Remember the words of Robert Frost: "No surprise in the writer, no surprise in the reader." A chapter-by-chapter, detailed outline simply isn't for everyone and might restrict or sap your creative drive when it comes time to actually draft the novel. Instead, generate a rough outline that highlights only the major conflicts and character interactions, essentially a more complex version of the summary you completed in Step 2. This big picture outline allows you to always have something exciting to write toward without eliminating the joy of discovering what your characters will do when left to their own devices.

I've created a template, located in Appendix F, to help you outline your novel and break down your writing schedule into manageable steps. If it's useful, plug your information into the template and go to town. If this kind of left-brain planning drives you bananas, however, consider yourself in good company. Approximately half of all published writers are called "pantsers," or writers who prefer writing by the seat of their pants rather than outlining. If this describes you, complete these first six steps in a fashion that feels more organic, planning to spend approximately four weeks on them before beginning the next step (Step 7, "Write the novel").

If, like me, you need the comfort and backbone of structure to really nail the story, I encourage you to use the template. I've filled out the first eight weeks of it below for *Eve* so you can see what it could look like. In my example, I have scheduled four weeks to finish the POP machine and eleven weeks to write the first third of the book. Notice that during several of those weeks, I chose to write multiple scenes. The system is set up so you can write one scene (approximately fifteen hundred words) a week and finish your novel in a year.

Also notice that I've included emotional memory and experiences that I'll be drawing on in writing each section. They're italicized in the table. Including these scene-level inspirations/models is crucial to writing with authenticity and heart. Other components of this template include

- Where I save my work. While I do all of my pre-novel work—essentially everything you've read in this book up until now—in a journal, I do the actual writing on a computer, and I save it in at least two different spots. I recommend you do the same so you never lose your work.

- What I'm reading as I'm writing because reading fiction inspires the writing of it.

- The fabulous but sometimes sucky ideas that inevitably strike as I embark on a creative venture.

- Roughly, which act the scene falls in, using Campbell's three-part departure-fulfillment-return structure.

- This one is big: how I treat myself when I reach a goal. Absolutely vital to the whole shebang. The process of writing itself is rewarding, but it doesn't always feel that way when you're sweating away in the fiction mines. Figure out what feels good—chocolate, bubble baths, a weekend in the woods—and make sure to tie rewards to commensurate work. I recommend a free, healthy reward for daily writing. I like to walk outdoors or watch my favorite TV show when I meet a daily reading or writing word count, for example. Save the big rewards, the ones that entail costs or calories, for big achievements, such as completing the POP method or drafting your novel's first act. Incorporating rewards is crucial to creating a work ethic but also to giving this undertaking the sense of adventure and excitement it deserves.

Rewrite Your Life Novel Template

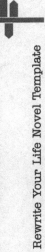

Week & Deadline	Pyramid on Point Step	Step Requirement	Location of Step	Read	Mark (x) When Done	Miscellaneous notes	Personal Reward When First Six Steps Are Complete
Week 1 (10/19/16)	Steps 1 & 2	Write one-sentence overview, then one-paragraph summary of book	*Eve* folder, saved in three locations	*Dark Dance*, Tanith Lee	X		Champagne, dark chocolate, and a full day of watching SyFy channel movies without guilt; also, without ever getting out of my pajamas. (Ah, who am I kidding? I never get out of my pajamas unless I'm forced to venture from the house. And by "pajamas," we both know I mean "big, dirty t-shirt," right? Isn't honesty the best? I get to be me, you get to be you.)
Week 2 (10/26/16)	Steps 3, 4, & 5	Create character bible, sketch main settings, and free-write ten minutes each for each sentence in one-paragraph summary	*Eve* folder, saved in three locations	*The Mysteries of Udolpho*, Radcliff	X		
Week 3 (11/2/16)	Step 6	Outline novel	Rewrite Your Life template, located in *Eve* folder, saved in three locations	*The Mysteries of Udolpho*, Radcliff	X	Strive to craft three discrete acts (past life, current life, future life), different tone in each.	
Week 4 (11/9/16)	Step 6	Outline novel	Rewrite Your Life template, located in *Eve* folder, saved in three locations	*Mistress of Mellyn*, Victoria Holt	X		

Week & Deadline	Scene/Conflict Personal Experience (If Any) I'm Drawing From	Scene goal/Emotional outcome/Tone Personal Experience (If Any) I'm Drawing From	Date & Setting	Reading Fiction (Mark X If So)	Word Count When Done	Act	Personal Reward After a Draft of Each Act Is Completed
Week 5 (11/16/16)	Eve arrives in Faith Falls, magic comes with her	Humor, poignancy, fear, show who the characters are / *Finding wedding ring on a shelf the morning after Jay's suicide*	Minnesota Summer 1907	X	4158	Act I Departure Act I must provide the inciting incident that sets the book in motion, introduces the novel's central conflict, and presents the main characters, showing rather than telling what the protagonist wants more than anything.	
Week 6 (11/23/16)	Crucifer Darkly's niece kills herself; town reacts peculiarly	Horror, confusion (break this scene up to reflect emotional explosion) / *Jay's mother's reactions to his suicide*	Minnesota Summer 1907	X	2619		
Week 7 (11/30/16)	Eve gets job at Ennis' clinic; they form a friendship; he warns her about Crucifer	Empathy, backstory on what type of parents she had and how she became who she is (break across three scenes) / *First dating Tony, unsure how to process his kindness*	Minnesota Summer 1907	X	1979		

Week & Deadline	Scene/Conflict Personal Experience (If Any) I'm Drawing From	Scene goal/Emotional outcome/Tone Personal Experience (If Any) I'm Drawing From	Date & Setting	Reading Fiction (Mark X If So)	Word Count When Done	Act	Personal Reward After a Draft of Each Act Is Completed
Week 8 (12/7/16)	Crucifer invites Eve to a party at his mansion *Attending rich friend's parents' party, feeling out of place, stilted conversation*	Romantic, but also unease, foreshadowing two worlds colliding	Minnesota Summer 1907 Darkly Manor	X	9049		
Week 9 (12/14/16)	Ennis invites Eve to his house for dinner; his mother cooks, comedy of errors *Dinner with poor cousins, Christmas 1986*	Humor, tenderness, empathy for Ennis, contrast to Crucifer	Minnesota Summer 1907 Ennis' farmhouse	X	1320		
Week 10 (12/21/16)	Darkly's niece's funeral *Jay's funeral*	Black humor, emotional distance, mystery of town's passivity	Minnesota Summer 1907 Faith Falls Cemetery	X	1777		
Week 11 (12/28/16)	Take this week off for the holidays; wrote multiple scenes week 8 to buy me a week off here						

Week & Deadline	Scene/Conflict Experience (If Any) I'm Drawing From	Scene goal/Emotional outcome/Tone Personal Experience (If Any) I'm Drawing From	Date & Setting	Reading Fiction (Mark X If So)	Word Count When Done	Act	Personal Reward After a Draft of Each Act Is Completed
Week 12 (1/4/17)	Darkly asks Eve to take over for his niece in caring for his children	Mystery, the cold lick of fear *Being hypnotized by carjacker in New Orleans*	Minnesota Summer 1907 Darkly Manor	X	1251		
Week 13 (1/11/17)	She moves into mansion; has nightmares; has destructive thoughts	Worry for her, mounting tension (break across several scenes) *Disorienting period following Jay's death, needing to work but feeling disconnected*	Minnesota Summer 1907 Darkly Manor	X	4476		
Week 14 (1/18/17)	She begins to get obsessive about finding truth about Darkly	Mounting tension, mystery, is she crazy or is there something there? *Searching through Jay's records*	Minnesota Summer 1907 Darkly Manor	X	5432		
Week 15 (1/25/17)	She confronts him, barging into room; he's playing innocently with his children	Discomfort at social failure. Major reversal; she thought she was figuring everything out, but now she doubts her sanity *Panic attacks in early 20s.*	Minnesota Summer 1907 Darkly Manor	X	1750		

End of Act I

My reward is one week of no writing, no guilt; read a Brené Brown book, get together with friends, one night away somewhere I've never been before, and visit the Humane Society to cuddle kittens.

The blank template in Appendix F includes spaces for you to schedule the writing of your entire novel, not just the first act. Also, that template includes three weeks for the editing phase. More to come on that.

STEP 7: WRITE THE NOVEL

This is it. The training wheels are off. You now have a snapshot of your novel and a rough map for creating it. You know which characters are populating your story, what they'll face, and in what locations they'll face it. Write one scene a week for forty-five weeks, each scene approximately seventeen hundred words, and you'll finish a complete first draft in less than a year.

Creating the first draft of your novel really is this straightforward—and the results are undeniably powerful—when you break it into these seven manageable steps. Using this method not only reduces much of the anxiety inherent in writing a book but also allows you to work out most of the snags and missteps from the get-go so you don't waste words or time when it comes to digging in and actually drafting the novel.

Remember to be gentle with yourself throughout. Also, watch for this Easter egg as you write truth-based fiction: because you are consciously organizing your crucible moments, you will find that you're buying yourself perspective and a precious few seconds to choose new reactions to old triggers. How cool is that?

 As you write your novel, continually draw on the emotions and experiences you mined in Chapter 5, "Choose Your Novel Concept."

Take me. The odds are good that being raised in a home of debauchery and secrecy coded me for my later mistakes. It attuned me to look past outward signs of success and stability to locate the deeply wounded. Essentially, I was a long-haired Burden Retriever, hard-wired to sniff out the unhealthiest person in the room to love and fix. Writing fiction based on my own experiences has bought me the self-awareness and safe space to instead heal *myself*. As a result, I no longer respond as readily to those childhood markers. Rewriting my life has also bestowed upon me a gnarly gratitude for the deepest of my wounds. How shallow would I be without them?

Rewriting my life didn't function as an on/off switch for learned behaviors but rather as an opportunity to choose based on who I want to be rather than what had happened to me. And who knows? When I finish writing *Eve*, I might even get to graduate to a new theme.

I wish the same for you, that by rewriting your life, you get to choose the theme that defines your journey on this earth. Use this chapter's seven steps to give you the necessary psychic distance from *your* story and create a safe, efficient structure for accessing the transformative, evocative power of writing fiction from your personal truths.

BONUS STEP

If you finish the first six steps of the POP method and still feel as if you're not quite ready to fly, try backward outlining the first three chapters of another novel. Any novel will work, as long as it is in the genre you'd like to write in. Let's say you want to write literary fiction, and so you select *The Secret Life of Bees*. Peel back the specifics—character, setting, time period—to reveal the rhythm of the story. This is what a backward outline might look like for the first three pages of that novel:

- Main character and three lines of setting on first page.

- Interaction between antagonist and protagonist on second page.

- Humor and foreshadowing on third page, followed by flashback.

- Inciting incident on fourth page.

And so on. After you create a backward outline of the first three chapters, slap your characters, setting, and time period onto that rhythm. Introduce *your* main character and describe your setting in three lines on your first page. On your second page, have your antagonist and protagonist interact. Once you have the structure of the first three chapters down, you're ready to sail.

One warning: make sure the central plot of your story is different from the novel you're backward outlining. For the first thriller I wrote, I backward outlined the first three chapters of *The Da Vinci Code* and slapped my own story onto that structure. My agent made me dramatically rework the first hundred pages. She said it was too much like *The Da Vinci Code*.

CHAPTER 10

THE MAGIC OF REVISION

One thing that helps is to give myself permission to write badly. I tell myself that I'm going to do my five or 10 pages no matter what, and that I can always tear them up the following morning if I want. I'll have lost nothing—writing and tearing up five pages would leave me no further behind than if I took the day off.

—Lawrence Block

I know some very great writers, writers you love who write beautifully and have made a great deal of money, and not one of them sits down routinely feeling wildly enthusiastic and confident. Not one of them writes elegant first drafts. All right, one of them does, but we do not like her very much.

—Anne Lamott

Many people hate to revise.

I *love* it.

It's my opportunity to take this lumpy, stinky thing I coughed up and transform it into a novel. All the heavy lifting is done. All that remains is to move some paintings around and decorate. Yay! Editing also allows me to see inside my own head. This seems counterintuitive because I wrote the book, so clearly I already know what it contains, right?

You'd be surprised.

Editing, for me, is an incredibly transformative stage of the turning fact-into-fiction process because during the writing period, you're releasing the story. During the editing stage, though, you're *rewriting* it. You get to mold it like clay, make it a different shape and color and texture, cut out what doesn't serve you, strengthen what you need more of, and generally seize control of the story, thereby commanding control of your life.

You become the boss of the narrative and, subsequently, your life.

If possible, give yourself a break between completing the first draft of your novel and editing it. I recommend at least two weeks during which you brag, celebrate, and make poor grocery choices. When you return to your manuscript, you'll see it with new eyes, which is literally what "re-vision" means.

You'll want to revise on two levels. One is content editing, which is big picture stuff. Maybe you have a character whom you discover doesn't bring anything to the narrative and you need to drop them. If you find yourself in this position, think about how to use that realization in your life. For example, I had a friend I shared a very formative period of my life with, but when we hit our forties, she no longer fit in the story I want to tell with my life. I wanted to live with more positivity and curiosity. She wanted to spend a lot of time living in the past and complaining about the present. After a few years of us choosing different directions, it became clear that remaining close friends didn't serve either of us. It was hard to step away from that friendship because we shared a past, and I love her. However, it was easier to put up a healthy boundary and end the relationship because I'd practiced cutting ill-fitting characters in my fiction.

Or, possibly you have a scene or chapter that isn't working or that needs to be moved. Hmm. Could the same be said of a habit or job that isn't fitting your life? Content editing takes care of this reorganization in your book and exercises the muscle that addresses the same in your life.

After you've done a round of content editing, you'll need to line edit. This is about dropping down to the sentence level and making sure there is constant flow. The life equivalent of line editing is literally looking for the best in each moment.

Content editing: big picture.

Line editing: sentence level.

They need to happen in that order, and both are necessary. Here's more detail on both and directions on how to apply them to your life.

CONTENT EDITING

You'll be unsurprised to learn that I have an acronym and an exercise to help you with content editing, which is also sometimes called substantive editing. I came up with it while drafting *Salem's Cipher*. The book's plot is complex, and the story is the longest I've ever written—over one hundred thousand words—with multiple points of view. Previously, I'd edited my manuscripts by giving myself a week or two off from them and then returning to read them straight through, noting inconsistencies and weak spots. This wouldn't work for editing *Salem's Cipher*. I needed to break that bad girl into scenes. Once I did that, I had to make sure every scene served a purpose and that they were organized in the best possible order.

Welcome to my brain, ARISE method.

I came up with this method while using Scrivener, software designed specifically for writing novels. Scrivener allows a writer to summarize each scene or chapter on a virtual notecard, move it around as necessary (thus moving the scene associated with it), and color-code or otherwise mark each scene. The ARISE method works just as well with old-school 3″ × 5″ notecards. Here's how it plays out. First, you summarize your book scene by scene, one scene per notecard. Make sure each card is numbered in the order that the scenes appear in your novel. Scene 1 notecard has a "1" in the corner, Scene 2 notecard has a "2" in the corner, and so on. Here's a sample notecard for the fifty-first scene of *Salem's Cipher:*

51

November 4, Senator Hayes gives a speech in Iowa. Show don't tell her policies, reinforce the type of tea she drinks because this detail is acted on in scene 67. When she begins speech, shots ring out.

If you want to buy colored notecards, I recommend taking this system one level deeper and assigning colors to the scenes as they make sense. If, for example, like me you have multiple viewpoints (*not* recommended for your first book), make all the scene cards from Character X's viewpoint pink, all the scene cards from Character Z's viewpoint blue, and so on. If, instead, your novel is heavy on subplot, make all the scene cards that deal with the main plot one color, and all the scenes that are more subplot-focused a different color.

Then, lay all your notecards out on the floor and jump right the hell into your book. I mean it. Get in there and move the cards around. Is there better flow if you do? Remove a card tied to a scene that has been bugging you. Does the book work better without it? Does each scene build on the one before it toward ever higher stakes? Are scenes intertwined, one inextricably connected to the next, or do they just sort of happen? If they appear disconnected from one another, how can you fix this issue?

Actually envision your story as a big movie playing around you or a symphony you're conducting. If you've color-coded your notecards, are the colors evenly distributed, or are they clotty and interrupting the flow? If they are overly clustered, rearrange. Is there a big hole somewhere in the narrative? Locate a blank notecard, scribble a scene summary on it, and see if it fills the void. Because you've numbered these notecards, you can always undo any changes quickly and cheaply, so be brave.

Go subterranean.

Once you have arranged, added, and deleted notecards in such a way that your narrative flows and is airtight with no missing or unnecessary scenes, it's time to ARISE. The foundation of this method is that every scene in your novel must serve at least one purpose. It must offer the reader

- Action
- Romance or Humor
- Information
- Suspense or
- Emotion

Obviously, the more the better, particularly if the only purpose the scene is currently serving is to provide information, which is the narrative equivalent of that guy who slows down to tell you that the store you're standing in front of, the only one in town that sells the widget you really need, is closed but will open again tomorrow at 9:00 a.m. He might be necessary, but wouldn't it be better if he was also being chased or was drop-dead gorgeous or leaves a mysterious clue behind or is holding a puppy?

Yes, of course.

Your job now is to go through each of your scene notecards, all still laid out in order (and if you've come up with a new order, pencil the updated numbers in the *lower right* corner, without erasing the original order you marked in the *upper left* corner), and scribble as many of the ARISE letters as pertain into the upper right corner of each notecard. If the scene has romance, pencil in an R. If it also has emotion, pencil in an E, and so on. If that scene has no letters, chuck it, no questions asked. If it fulfills only one letter, consider what you can add to it to give it at least two. Write a note to yourself on that card about what you're going to add to that scene. If a notecard has earned at least three letters, it's golden.

I'll give you an example from *Salem's Cipher*.

CONTENT EDITING

Here is scene 51, the same scene summarized in the notecard sample I shared. It is written from the point of view of Senator Gina Hayes, presidential candidate, who Salem does not yet know has the power to save it. Senator Hayes is about to give a speech in Iowa.

> Gina Hayes looked up from her schedule. "Matthew, has someone tested the teleprompters?"
>
> "Yes, but you won't need them." Matthew didn't pause his typing to answer but did stop to issue a threat to the cable news anchor creeping closer to Hayes despite multiple warnings. With a single gesture, he also managed to get her pre-speech chamomile tea brought to her.
>
> Hayes smiled as she sipped. American voters were worried they'd be electing Gina and her husband to run the country when in fact, they should be worried about the package deal of Gina and her assistant. Matthew had chosen her outfit (a slimming pantsuit in deep "power" red), her hair ("less of the matronly Martha, more Assertive Annie with a dash of Sexy Susie"), and her make-up ("*Chop chop!* I need her to look like she's actually slept since last May"). Hayes had chosen the content of her speech, however, and

written most of it through the night, working with her team of speech writers.

The address hit the three points she'd based her campaign on: economic power, global stability, and environmental protection. This one also contained an Easter egg, something her speech writers had begged her not to include: a nod to the so-called kitchen table issues that had been so important to her as a law student in college and continued to define her. She would address women's reproductive freedom, gay rights, income inequality, the pay gap, the minimum wage, immigration reform, veteran's rights.

She would represent the people.

"Are you ready?" Matthew held his iPad in one hand and her mobile mic in the other.

Hayes nodded briskly and handed him the empty tea cup. "Always."

Matthew appeared wistful for a moment.

"What is it?" Hayes asked.

"I hate to say it, but Charming Charlie was right. You look beautiful."

Hayes actually laughed, a ruby-colored chuckle seldom heard in public. "You're not getting a raise, Matthew."

He winked and stepped away, the melancholy smile still on his face. Hayes was escorted into the wide open arena, the applause deafening. Tens of thousands of people jumped to their feet, screaming, waving signs, some of them crying. Hayes walked to the center of the stage and held her hands in the air. The teleprompters to her left and right were suspended like thin prisms. The space heaters on the stage created a visible barrier against the frigid November air, a wavy storm front that Hayes had to stare through like a mirage to see her audience.

But it didn't matter. This is where she was supposed to be. These were the people she was fighting for. She let the cheers wash over her.

"Thank you for inviting me to your lovely stadium, Hawkeyes!"

Impossibly, the volume of the cheers rose.

Hayes' smile widened.

<u>She had her mouth open to begin her speech when the first shot rang out, popping like a car backfire, the bullet piercing the mirage of the stage.</u>

<u>Two Secret Service agents were on top of Senator Gina Hayes' body before the second shot was fired.</u>

This example has **Suspense** (underlined) because you don't know if she lives or dies. It also provides important character Information (in gray), and so it technically was good enough. I wanted this book to be better than good enough, though. I also wanted the **E**, emotion, because I need readers to feel something for this character so it matters that she's in danger. And I wanted the **R**, romance or humor (in this case, more humor), because when I laid the notecards out, I realized the book hadn't had any **R** for a while, and as a result, it was growing dense. To revise, I first updated the notecard like this:

> 51 RISE
>
> November 4, Senator Hayes gives a speech in Iowa. Foreground relationship with husband to create poignancy, humanize her; include spark of humor. Show don't tell her policies, reinforce the type of tea she drinks because this detail is acted on in scene 67. When she begins speech, shots ring out.

Then, I wrote the following and tacked it on to the opening of the scene. I've highlighted the humor in italics and the emotion in bold.

"You look beautiful."

"Charles, it's the new millennium. Don't you mean I look powerful? Smart? Capable?" **But Senator Gina Hayes' broad smile showed she was teasing. Her husband always said exactly the right thing. It was one of his gifts.**

"I mean it." He pulled her into an embrace rare enough that Matthew Clemens stopped juggling seven different appointments, hundreds of texts and emails, and a phone conversation with CNN to stare, agape. The three of them were backstage at Kinnick Stadium on the University of Iowa campus. Outside, an unusually plump crescent moon was crawling up the night sky, and the winter-washed air carried ice currents that nipped at noses and fingers. That didn't keep the record crowd of 35,000 supporters from bundling in parkas, hats, and scarves to hear a historic speech by who looked to be the first female president of the United States of America.

The election was in 6 days. News stations were predicting the highest voter turnout in history. Technicians, news crews, and security personnel bustled backstage. Since no moment of Senator Hayes life was private, at least two different cable stations were showing a live feed of her husband's embrace. She knew this, or at least guessed.

She didn't care.

She was going to steal these five seconds in her husband's arms, safe, grounded, a blink of selfishness before she stepped in front of thousands, millions with television and the Internet, and gave them everything she had. She'd been raised in the ideal of public service, taught by her father George that your life only had meaning if it helped others. She'd seen the sacrifices he'd made right up until his death of a heart attack two years earlier. She knew how proud he'd be of her, and that was one of the sparks that kept her fire burning.

Hayes pulled out of her husband's arms, letting her hand linger on his cheek for a moment. "Do I still look okay?"

He flashed the charming smile that had disarmed men and women—too many women—his entire political career. "You've never looked more powerful, smart, or capable." He leaned close to her ear and whispered. "And I've never seen you look more beautiful. If you need help getting out of that suit later, you know where to find me."

With a wink, he stepped back and let her hair and make-up crew complete their final touches. Hayes threw him one last glance before returning to work, wondering how he could still surprise her, still make her feel so attractive, even after all these years.

With those additions, the scene now included four of the five ARISE components: Romance/Humor, Information, Suspense, and Emotion. I knew I could move on to the next scene.

 As another example, refer to Appendix E and check out Cisneros' scenes for The House on Mango Street. *Every single scene in the book contains at least three of the ARISE components. There is emotion and information in every one of them plus humor in most and action, suspense, or romance in some. That's one of the reasons this book reads so well.*

Once you've marked each card's ARISE status for your own story, step back one last time. Is all the romance or humor crammed into one act like it had been in my book before I expanded on scene 51? If so, spread it out.

Is the first scene written to elicit an emotional response from a reader? If not, make a note on the card how you will fix that. One trick is to have at least one person stressed or off balance in the opening scene.

Have you been led to believe that your novel doesn't need action or suspense because it's literary fiction? Consider that action is story movement and that there is suspense in the evolution of a human (will they make a different choice this time?), and find quiet ways to make sure you have both throughout.

How fun is the ARISE method? *FUN.*

Once you've created the notecards, subsequently reorganized the story, and then done an ARISE check for each scene, compile the note-cards in order and restructure your manuscript as necessary. The good news about content editing is that if you've applied the information in this book, you will have much less content editing to do than someone who just sat down to write. You'll have a map and a compass and will have worked out the major kinks before you even hit the road.

Still, even the most skilled drafter regularly cuts scenes and adds others. The best piece of advice I ever received on this front came from my friend, author and *Boston Globe* reviewer Hallie Ephron, who told me to keep a Saver file for each novel I write. I paste the scenes that I can't use into that file. It makes me feel better about slashing my darlings. I've used some of those Savers for short stories, but mostly, once they're out of the book and I've had a couple days to mourn, I realize they were crap to begin with.

LINE EDITING

I almost enjoy the line editing more than content editing. In line editing, you get to shine your jewelry, tightening your words and streamlining your sentences, making sure the story flows and glows. Besides putting the polish on something you've worked so hard on, line editing is also one of the few places in writing a novel where the rules are non-negotiable. The first requirement is that you must read your entire book out loud. It's weird, but trust me, you have to do it; our ears are much better proofreaders than our eyes. When reading out loud, you are listening for consistency in tone and voice, variety in sentence length, a hook at the end of each chapter, infrequent and well-chosen dialogue tags, conciseness, and correct spelling and grammar. I provide a handy checklist of these line editing require-ments, including examples, at the end of this chapter.

OUTSIDE EDITING

If you elect not to publish this book or will be distributing to only a handful of close friends, applying the line editing checklist is plenty enough tweaking. If you intend to publish, however, you need one more level of editing before you send your book into the world: outside editing.

How this type of editing looks depends on your temperament and budget. Take me. I'm an introvert with more money than personality. Ha! That's only half true. I don't have a lot of money. But the idea of joining a writer's group of strangers is off-putting to me. That's why I hire a professional editor, a brilliant woman who lives in Oregon. She was referred to me by a New York City agent when I was shopping around my first novel. This agent promised that I was close and that if I worked with an editor, I'd push the manuscript over the top. She was right, and I've worked with the same professional for every book since.

There are wonderful editors available, and the best way to find them is to ask other writers for recommendations. This book's last chapter offers tips for meeting writers. If budget is an issue, if you are a social person, or if you simply like to workshop your writing (which is a valuable endeavor when you have a good critique group), I recommend joining or forming a writers group. You can locate one by searching online, putting out a call on social media, or by contacting your local library or college writing department. I've never belonged to one, but I am friends with successful authors who swear by their writing group, and I believe if you find or create a gang that's a good fit, it'll rocket your writing to the next level.

After all is said and done, let this editing process be a relief and a celebration.

In fiction as in life, what we throw away is at least as important as what we keep. Take charge of your story. Toss out what no longer serves it. Revel in what remains. Editing, more than any other part of the writing process, is psychological weightlifting. It's the push and pull between the story we think other people want to hear and the story down in our bones that we know we must tell. Our job is to get out of our own way and not clutter up the process with flowery words or inauthentic plot twists or overwrought love stories.

We have to peel away the noise to reveal the tale we're meant to tell.

I'm going to leave you with a story that best exemplifies this. A couple years ago, I had the pleasure of killing time in a green room with the legendary Sue Grafton, a tiny woman with a delightfully sharp tongue, author of the best-selling Kinsey Millhone series. Sue was a screenwriter before penning her first novel, and based on her terrible experiences, she's famously claimed that she will never sell her series to Hollywood (and believe me, they've asked) and will haunt her children if they defy that wish after she dies.

We were talking about the love/hate relationship we have with writing and where story ideas come from. She pulled out some Jungian psychology that has stuck with me ever since.

"Our stories come from shadow," she said. "At least the ones worth telling."

I nodded knowingly, but she's nobody's idiot and could see I had no clue what she was talking about.

"Shadow is our dark side, that bloody gunk that we're embarrassed about but that we all possess, the source of our inspiration and our evil. Our ego wants to steer the story, wants to tell us the book we're writing is wonderful and great and the world needs it, or that it's horrible and better never see the light of day. It's our shadow that we must listen to, though. Our shadow cuts through the crap and tells the truth. It's our job as writers to listen to it."

Find your shadow and respect its whispers. The rewards you'll reap extend far beyond the written page.

LINE EDITING CHECKLIST

Check for these requirements as you read your book out loud, line editing as you go.

Requirement	Check If Met
Sentence length varies.	
Each chapter ends with a hook, regardless of genre.	
There are no information dumps. Backstory and insight are woven throughout the book.	
When possible, movement takes the place of dialogue tags. EXAMPLE: Instead of: "What are you doing here?" she asked. Use: She dropped her coffee cup. "What are you doing here?"	
When dialogue tags must be used for clarity, use "said" in almost all cases, replacing adverbs with action. EXAMPLE: Instead of: "No one ever listens to me," Phil pouted angrily. Use: "No one ever listens to me," Phil said, slapping the table.	
The voices are consistent. For example, if your protagonist is an eight-year-old who normally curses like a sailor but she starts talking like she's in church while she's with her friends, you've lost her voice. Get it back.	
The tone is uniform. For example, if you have crafted a dark horror novel and the main character is being hunted, don't have him run into the grocery store for a Coke and some RedVines unless you are writing a deliberate parody. Otherwise, keep the tones consistent, transitioning consciously from one to another.	

Requirement	Check If Met
You use specific, descriptive language when possible. EXAMPLE Instead of: He had clothes on. Use: He wore a military jacket. Make sure not to overdo this one. A writer needs to be invisible to the reader, using the fewest, clearest words possible to convey the scene.	
All the words are necessary to move the story forward.	
Any research is accurate.	
Your verb tense is consistent, either all in past tense or all in present tense.	
You've eliminated "crutch" words. These are words you overuse. Mine are "just" and "a couple," to give you just a couple examples.	
In most cases, make each sentence an active construction, which is more exciting to read and clearer. Basically, make sure it's clear at the beginning of the sentence who is doing the thing. EXAMPLE Instead of: The cherries and the blueberries were Sam's favorite fruits. Use: Sam's favorite fruits were cherries and blueberries.	
Grammar errors are either used deliberately in dialogue or deleted. You don't have to be a grammar expert to catch most of your errors as long as you're reading out loud. Your ear knows.	
Spell check. And never entirely trust the machine. Example: that one time spell check thought "I got all my dicks in a row" was a perfectly kosher sentence to send to a colleague.	

171

PART III

YOUR TRANSFORMATION

PART III

YOUR
TRANSFORMATION

CHAPTER 11

A DAY IN THE LIFE

Be ruthless about protecting writing days, i.e., do not cave in to endless requests to have "essential" and "long overdue" meetings on those days. The funny thing is that, although writing has been my actual job for several years now, I still seem to have to fight for time in which to do it.

—*J. K. Rowling*

You might not write well every day, but you can always edit a bad page. You can't edit a blank page.

—*Jodi Picoult*

A word after a word after a word is power.

—*Margaret Atwood*

There is no greater agony than bearing an untold story inside you.

—*Maya Angelou*

When I was four, my dad sat my sister and me down. He probably had a drink in one hand and a well-packed bong in the other. I can't remember. I do remember his earnestness, though, and the confidence in his words.

"You know you can be anything you want to be when you grow up, right?" His bloodshot eyes traveled from my sister to me. "*Anything.*"

My sister's face lit up. She's always been the nice one, full of hope and drive and kindness. I think she said she wanted to be a doctor or maybe a dancer. Whatever it was, dad nodded approvingly and turned his boozy eyes toward me. "Jess, you're next. You can be *anything*. ANYTHING. So, what do you want to be when you grow up?"

I paused for effect. "I want to be a cat."

I wasn't being a smart-ass. For once, I was actually picking up what he was putting down: I could be *anything*. My parents consistently instilled this faith in me, a belief in my ability and right to navigate and choose my life. That gift has given me a crazy, hairy confidence that I can craft a novel, despite the many detours, pickpockets, and bad weather I've encountered on the journey. Maybe you don't have that brand of assurance, but you do have me, here on the other side, holding out my hand to help you across the stream of fire.

So listen.

This writing isn't for the complacent, the unkind, the arrogant. It's for those of us who want to clear our dusty junk piles of shame and fear so we can live rich, plump, laugh-out-loud lives. It is hard work. There will be days you will want to quit. There will be minutes inside of days when you want to quit. There will be ten straight seconds when you think you have it all figured out followed by a whole hot day when you wonder who the hell you thought you were because you can't even keep your bathroom clean let alone write a novel.

Case in point. I have a friend who was all fired up to write his first book. He's an English professor and definitely has the chops. It started out great. He had himself on a five-hundred-word-a-day diet.

That lasted for *one* day.

On the second day, he realized he hadn't cleaned the grout in his bathroom for a while. He took care of that urgent issue, assuring himself he'd get back on track the next day. Day three, he was astonished to discover that his fridge hadn't been cleaned out in weeks. He put out that fire before going to bed, relieved that he'd taken care of it and confident he'd get back on track with the writing the next day. You know how this story ends, right? He told me it got so bad that instead of writing his self-prescribed five hundred words for the day, he varnished all his kitchen cupboards.

He doesn't even own the house he lives in.

That's how ugly this may get.

If this ninja level of procrastination happens to you, forgive yourself, and write the next day. Do that as many times as you need to, but not too many times. Set small goals and claim small rewards, all of which lead up to the ultimate goal and a reward beyond your wildest dreams: a complete novel, one worth reading and most definitely worth the time it took to write.

Use the steps in Chapter 9 to establish small goals. Stick to them and make sure to reward yourself when you meet them. The scale of what you are attempting will crush you if you don't keep the goals consistent and attainable, and you'll be demoralized if you don't reward yourself. But some days, even that won't be enough. On those days, you will want beer, courage, and a kitten to get you through. I recommend you borrow a kitty or volunteer at your local animal shelter and get back to work, scheduling your writing life in a manner that makes sense to you.

Here's how that looks for me.

I get up before 6:00 a.m. to ready my kids for school. Once they're out the door, I walk the dog and pick up the house. If I'm feeling ridiculous, I work out on a big blue ball. Then, I get myself ready for my teaching job and spend the next six to eight hours leading classes, grading, and prepping. I return home, start supper and clean some more, and spend the afternoon and evening hanging out with my family, helping with homework, and playing Ultimate Ping Pong.

At around 8:00 p.m., I write. If you think I'm tired, you're damn right. I used to give myself a time limit. I had to sit in that chair for two hours. What I discovered is that if I'm working within a time limit, "research" becomes super important to me. I suddenly *must* head to Wikipedia to unearth the governor of Minnesota the year it became a state, and awfulplasticsurgery.com to decide what procedures I should avoid when I land the big writing contract, and to Pinterest to research decorating tips for my latest protagonist. If I'm feeling particularly low, I'll head to Amazon to check my sales numbers.

These days, I set a word limit. I'm not allowed out of the chair until I write two thousand words. I came up with that number because I am a fast writer (thanks to the POP method), and it's a reasonable number for me. Set your word count at a level that makes sense to you, the one you selected in your timeline, but do not get out of your seat until you've met it. Use your own exhaustion, your own desire to be done, as an inherent reward. Toss in a little Facebook time or watching your favorite TV show or reading an awesome book as your pot of gold at the end of the words. Maybe it works better for you to switch this schedule around and write in the morning or over lunch.

That's fine.

Just don't buy into the concept of writer's block. My friend, the *New York Times* best-selling author Reed Farrel Coleman, sputters when people mention writer's block. "You ever heard of 'accountant's block'? 'Firefighter's block'? 'Waitress' block'? No! Just do your damn job."

Yup.

Some days you'll do better than others, and some hours will be more fun than the ones before them, but you still do it, one day after the next. Worry about perfection during the editing phase. For now, just pin the words to paper.

Watch your self-awareness grow.

Feel your self-esteem strengthen.

Smile as your word count goes up, up, and up.

If you get stuck, or are not sure which way the story needs to turn, hold that question in your brain until the answer comes. A handy tool for thinking yourself out of a narrative corner is the Silva glass of water technique. Here's how it works. Immediately before you go to sleep, grab your journal, a pen, and a full glass of water, placing all three within reach of your bed. Drink half the glass of water with your eyes closed. While drinking, envision the narrative snarl that needs untangling and assure yourself that you will find the solution.

Return the half-full glass of water to your nightstand and go to sleep. You may wake up in the middle of the night with a solution, or it may come to you when you wake up in the morning. If it does, write it down *immediately*. If it doesn't, drink the rest of the glass of water the next morning with your eyes closed. While you do, muse over that blasted snarl that needs fixing and assure yourself that you will find the solution.

It might take a day or two, but this method never fails. I think it works like a meditation in that it distracts you enough to get out of your own way. Sue Grafton might tell you that it allows you to muzzle your ego so you can hear your shadow. If your shadow speaks to you when you're writing, listen, even if it feels like more work, or like you're going to have to let go of a character or plot twist that you love. Smother your ego with a pillow. A big part of the rewards of novel writing is that it puts you in touch with your instincts, so don't fight this ego-out, shadow-in process.

If you're still stuck after the Silva method, it's a sign that you're worried about something else. Usually, that something is what someone or the whole world will think of your writing. The writer Erica Jong, author of the semi-autobiographical *Fear of Flying*, which has sold over twenty million copies, once said, "I went for years not finishing anything. Because, of course, when you finish something you can be judged." If you're worried about being judged, and anyone who says they aren't is a liar, remind yourself that no one has to see this book but you. Your job is to get the words on paper. Don't borrow worry.

I also recommend keeping a copy of Steven Pressfield's The *War of Art* handy. It's a slim book, available at any library. Pressfield explains better than anyone the internal battle with writing, and more importantly, outlines why it's worth fighting, day after day. My first novel came out in 2006, and it is still a daily struggle for me to write. Daily. Battle. And I fight it over and again, never regretting it because once I push over the hill and land in the pool of words, I feel like I'm in the right place at the right time, without fail.

Writing makes me wholly present in this world.

It will do the same for you.

While novel writing is an inherently rewarding experience, and writing fiction is a naturally gentle vehicle for accessing memory and experience, crafting a full-length book can be a daunting process, particularly when you are probing your most challenging experiences to harvest the raw materials.

But writing is important.

In the end, it's not about making the time to write. It's about making the writing important to you. We all make time for what matters to us.

I recommend, as part of this soul journey, that you make time for other writers, as well. Passionate, haunted people who have struggled but yet choose creativity are the best souls to have in your life. They can handle accidental farts and irrational fears and ludicrous thoughts. They are the lifeguards of the common psyche. By drowning and coming back to tell us what's down there, they save the rest of us the pain.

Love them.

Play with them.

You'll need them.

Writing is often dark, heavy work, even if you're writing comedy. Don't trust a novelist who says writing books is easy, by the way. If you must trust them, at least pinch them first, and then come hang out with the rest of us, because the tribe is waiting for you.

To find your creative community, start by looking for a writing center in your area. If you're in a big city, you will certainly have one, like The Loft in Minneapolis or the Lighthouse Writers Workshop in Denver. Sign up for a class or just hang out in their coffee shop. Start putting out feelers, letting people know you're writing, and see what opportunities to gather with other writers pop up. Search for writing groups online.

Check out writing conferences in your area and consider joining one of the major writing organizations to streamline the process of connecting with your people. Choose based on the genre of the novel you're currently writing: Science Fiction and Fantasy Writers of America if you're writing sci-fi, for example, or Romance Writers of America if you're writing romance. They all have excellent websites with more information. Even if you are an introvert like me, you'll find that when you locate your tribe, it's even better than being alone.

Because you've made the commitment to write, you've already chosen creativity. All that's left is to track down the other people who've done the same. It's glorious when you find them. The Buddhist nun Pema Chödrön writes about cultivating the kindness and bravery it takes to leave a rut and begin to relate to discomfort, compassion, and joy. She calls it living like a warrior, and it is. Find the people who are doing the same, and watch your writing and your personal evolution deepen.

Then, open your door to magic. Should I have confessed at the beginning of this book that I believe in magic? Saved you some time? If you've already begun writing, though, you know it's true: we can make magic. You can pile up letters to build words that create worlds. Just by scribbling in a notebook or typing on a keyboard, you transport yourself to somewhere no one has ever been. If your writing is good, you can do the same for others. Anne Lamott says it best:

> What a miracle it is that out of these small, flat, rigid squares of paper unfolds world after world after world, worlds that sing to you, comfort and quiet or excite you. Books help us understand who we are and how we are to behave. They show us what community and friendship mean; they show us how to live and die. (15)

But that's not the magic I'm referring to right now, though it is a mystical thing. I'm not even talking about the alchemy of transforming your fears, joys, and sadness into gold, though that's awesome as well.

When I say there is magic in writing, I'm talking about that moment when you know you've tapped into something bigger than yourself, and it's like you're simply taking notes as someone tells you the story. Psychologist Mihály Csíkszentmihályi calls it flow, that state where we are so immersed, so focused, that the real world falls away. Some Eastern religions refer to it as a meditative state. You've maybe heard it as "hitting your groove" or "catching the wave."

It's the feeling of being in absolutely the right place at the right time.

Nothing beats it.

If you write, you will find yourself in the flow of the universe.

That is magic.

I have a bag of gorgeous glass marbles the size of superballs in deep cloud colors, and I tuck them outdoors to thank the story fairies when I hit the flow. That's how happy it makes me. Don't get me wrong. I love my kids and my man and my friends and family, and they're important to me. It's just that nothing makes me feel alive like writing.

To illustrate this, I'm going to end with a story.

I keep a journal by my bed so I can jot down ideas that come to me in the middle of the night. I used to tell myself I'd remember these sleeping inspirations, but I never did. The only way to snare them, I found, was to remove as many obstacles as possible to writing them down. Hence, the dream journal.

It'd been a lean couple years for that journal. At least it had been until this particular week. I was woken in the middle of the night by the best idea for a book I'd ever had. My heart was thumping. This idea was so solid that I didn't even play the "you sure it's worth leaving the warmth of the covers?" game my shabby ego loves to toss around. I shot up and grabbed my notepad. I scratched down the idea. I fell back into bed, my heartbeat still pounding pleasantly. The smile stayed on my face until the next morning, when I promptly forgot I'd even had a dream. I went about my day, content to live a mediocre life, when I remembered.

The dream.

The story idea that would rock the world.

I couldn't remember any details, just that I had written it down. Unfortunately, I was now at work.

I had to wait two more agonizing hours until I could go home and see what I'd written.

When I returned to my house, I rushed to the journal and tore it open to the page where I'd written the dream.

It held three lines of dialogue:

MAN: I have a writing potato.

WOMAN: What's a writing potato?

MAN: Yukon gold.

That was it.

Goddammit, that was it.

Do you see what I'm saying here? Don't take yourself too seriously. This process is transformative and ridiculous and will make your life better, but it's still your life. Enjoy it. Clear out the junk pile/grief/shame so you have room to live fully because here's a fact about problems: you deal with them now or you deal with them later. They never disappear on their own, and the longer you wait to address them, the more people they affect. But keep on celebrating and being curious as you alchemize your pain into art.

After you write your novel and reprocess your mental junk into something cohesive and therapeutic, you might realize that your passion lies elsewhere, somewhere other than writing books. Celebrate this new knowledge, and follow your passion. It's absolutely fine if novel writing was not intended to be your career but rather a stop for you on your journey, a chance to unload some bags so you can travel lighter to where you're supposed to be. You can always return to novel writing if you find the bags accumulating again.

In the end, writing *May Day* (the title makes sense now, doesn't it?) allowed me to see Jay's death for the gruesome, gnarly gift it was. Without it, I probably wouldn't have become a writer, and I certainly wouldn't have met the love of my life. Could I just have met Tony at eighteen and lived happily ever after? No, because I had to work through the crap of growing up the daughter of an alcoholic Vietnam vet who was fighting and continues to fight PTSD. Could I just have been raised in a happy, mellow house? Yeah, but then I'd be Dull City, Iowa.

What you've experienced so far, it's all part of the ride. Distill it into a kick-ass novel first to give yourself practice in steering and spinning your story and second maybe to heal, inspire, or just plain entertain someone else as they go on theirs.

Write.

Rewrite.

Then live.

Afterword

Publishing a book does not make you a writer.

Writing a book makes you a writer.

When you are done rewriting your life, when you are able to see this representation of your personal transformation in novel form, you will feel an immense satisfaction. You will understand that the healing is in the writing of the story, not the sharing of it.

That said, some of you may want to explore publishing at the end of this healing process, and it'd be irresponsible for me not to share what I know. I will sidestep an "art for art's sake" discussion, even though I believe strongly in the inherent value of living a creative life. I won't even delve any further into the established physical and mental health benefits of creativity, particularly creative writing, as I've already covered that in depth. Rather, I'm going to give you three publishing options to explore if you so choose:

- Snap publishing
- Traditional publishing
- Self-publishing

SNAP PUBLISHING

In snap publishing you type your manuscript, content- and then line-edit it, have at least one other person give you feedback, and then upload it to Kindle (e-book) and/or CreateSpace (paperback book).

Snap.

You now have created a book that anyone with Internet access and a credit card can buy. They likely *won't* buy it, because your book will be one fish in a sea of 129,864,880, and they won't be able to find it.

That's why you should never snap publish unless you have a specific, very small audience in mind for your manuscript, and they're okay with it in whatever form it comes. An example is a compilation of your grandmother's recipes woven with family stories that you'd like to gift to your aunts for the holidays or a collection of poems that you wrote for your significant other.

The only other reason to snap publish—and the most important one, if you ask me—is that this was a novel you needed to write for yourself. For a million excellent reasons, it was essential you get this story on paper, and you now want it to be bound and on a shelf so you can walk by it and be reminded of how amazing you are and how committed to doing a little better every day and how important creativity is to you. So, you upload your file to CreateSpace, create a cover, order yourself a few sample copies, and never list your book for sale to the public.

This tangible celebration of your accomplishment is a perfect reason, the very best reason, to snap publish your book, and please, if we ever cross paths, tell me what you did so I can buy you chocolate and have the pleasure of knowing you are in this world.

TRADITIONAL PUBLISHING

The traditional publishing industry hasn't changed much in the four-hundred-plus years since *Don Quixote* was published, though distribution may have evolved a bit. Cervantes' publisher, Francisco de Robles, sent most of the four hundred first editions of the book via ship to the Americas, where he was hoping for a better price. A shipwreck near La Havana claimed all but seventy. Now, as in Cervantes' time, the author writes the book, acquires a publisher, and the publisher assumes all costs, including providing editing, printing, marketing, and distribution services in exchange for a generous cut of the profits.

Up until a few decades ago, you could even send your manuscript directly to publishers and ask if they'd be interested in it. Now, around 80 percent of fiction projects, maybe more, require a literary agent. These professionals serve as gatekeepers for publishing houses.

Here's how the traditional publication route looks from the author's perspective, from idea to ISBN:

1. Write book.

2. Revise, fine-tune, and edit book.

3. Hire a professional editor.

4. Query appropriate agents.

5. Acquire agent.

6. Agent queries appropriate publishing houses.

7. Receive publishing contract. (Yay! Yayyayayay! Big celebration time!)

8. Sign contract and receive advance against future sales, as negotiated by your agent. Plan on receiving 10 to 15 percent of the book's wholesale price (wholesale price is approximately half the cost of cover price), and bank on 15 percent of *that* going directly to your agent. What you receive after the advance is known as royalties, and royalties are mailed out twice a year after your advance has earned out.

9. Your publisher creates a publication schedule, which usually results in your book being published one year, give or take, after you sign the contract. This involves the art department designing a cover, an editor working with you to polish the manuscript, a copywriter crafting the back cover copy, publicity sending the manuscript to reviewers and (if you're lucky) setting up interviews and possibly a book tour, and the marketing department working on the distribution plan.

10. Your book is released.

You'll notice how very little you control in this process. Other than writing the best book you can, making sure it is professionally edited before you send it out, and querying the appropriate agents in a professional and engaging manner, there's nothing you can do to acquire a publishing contract except possibly making a sex tape and, some days, that honestly doesn't seem like my worst idea.

To land an agent, you need to locate all those who are looking to represent novels in the genre you've written in. This can be done a number of ways, but I recommend these three:

- Look in the acknowledgments section of some of your favorite books in the genre you've written in. Authors often thank their agents. This route works well for two reasons. One, you know this agent is good because they landed this author a contract. Two, when you query that agent, you can compare your writing style/chosen genre to that of their client whose book you read.

- Check out the Association of Author Representatives web page. This is free and awesome because all the agents on it have been vetted. They're above board. This means that they don't make any money unless they make money for you. This is how it should always be, but there are unscrupulous agents out there. Don't ever sign with one who asks you for up-front payment; they should only be earning a percentage of your royalties, nothing more.

- Check into the Literary Market Place. LMP is a paid service, so visit your local library to see if it has a subscription.

Once you've got a list of at least fifty potential agents, none of them in the same agency, query them. The query letter, which is almost always sent via email these days, should contain these parts:

- An attention-getter that includes the name, genre, and word count of your novel. "Imagine you're walking down a dark alley, and you feel a hot breath on your back. You have a millisecond to decide to run or fight. My 84,000-word horror novel, *Poe's Perils*, deals with those moments between paralysis and power."

- A one- or two-sentence synopsis of your novel. This is hard for many people, but since you already completed Step 1 of the POP method outlined in Chapter 9, all you have to do is pull that sentence into your query letter.

- A comparison between your book and other, similar books that are bestsellers. This establishes the marketability of your novel. "Fans of Stephen King and Sarah Pinborough will be drawn to *Poe's Perils* fast pacing and intelligent gore."

- Any publishing experience you have. If you have none, no worries. Seriously. Every author lacked publishing experience at one time in their life.

- The offer to send the completed manuscript upon request.

Short and sweet. That's it, unless the agent specifically requests more. This is a good time to underscore that you should send the agent *only* what they request and also *be sure* to send the agent exactly what they request. Proofread your query, too, and if you can, have a smart and generous friend proofread it for you. Successful agents receive hundreds of query letters a week. Your polished gem must demonstrate that you're professional by respecting the agent's time and talent.

Then, you wait.

While you wait, I'll offer you this sadly inspirational tale that's shaped kinda like a turd but smells more like a pep talk. A pep turd. It took me over four hundred queries to land an agent for *May Day*. I'd haul fifty query letters to the post office because this was 2003, and we didn't even have dial-up where I lived. Those rejections would start flooding in, and I'd send out fifty more queries. Every now and again I'd get a word of encouragement or suggestions for revision and resubmission, and I'd always edit if the feedback made sense.

Mostly, though, I received a short rejection, sometimes printed on half sheets: "Sorry, but no."

Like, I wasn't even worth a whole piece of paper.

After 423 rejections, I acquired my first agent, a woman with a side business selling crystals in Colorado. You could literally click one part of her website for her agent page, and another click would land on a photo of her wearing fringy suede and balancing rose quartz and tiger's eye on her open palms. But damn, she looked good to someone who'd been rejected over four hundred times. She didn't sell my book, and we parted ways amicably after six months. My next agent sold *May Day* and *June Bug* in a two-book deal.

Slow and steady—with a healthy dollop of self-awareness and willingness to revise if the rejections show a pattern—wins this race.

Not catchy, not quick, but true.

SELF-PUBLISHING

The third option is self-publishing, which I believe you should try only if you've exhausted all traditional publishing options. Remember how many books are out there? Nearly 130 million. It's difficult to be heard in all that noise without a publishing company with an in-house publicity and marketing team to help you. Plus, when you don't have the street cred a traditional publisher bestows, it's a challenge to get your book reviewed, let alone onto store shelves.

That said, if you've tried the traditional route and it didn't bear fruit, or you're already traditionally published and want to become a hybrid author, then self-publishing might be for you, and it can be incredibly lucrative if you treat it like the job it is.

Self-publishing allows for more diverse authors to be heard, more experimental and niche content to be written and read, and for traditionally published authors to gain more control over their careers. Indie e-book sales eclipsed the Big Five publishers' sales on Amazon for the first time in 2015. Self-publishing is not going away, and its increasing power and popularity have created an exciting and challenging time for readers, writers, and writing organizations.

I have firsthand experience self-publishing *The Catalain Book of Secrets*. I received a lot of confusing rejections, crazy praise for the book followed by a big, ugly, unsupported "but." This is a book I love, a deeply personal fictionalization of lifelong traumas. My freelance editor and agent both adored it. It got close to finding a home in the big houses, but ultimately, it was rejected by every one of them. I was heartbroken, but I wasn't willing to let this novel die on the vine.

I chose self-publishing.

It's important to underscore that self-publishing is an entirely different beast from snap publishing. Snap publishing is a modern version of going to Kinko's and having something you've written bound. In self-publishing an individual takes on all the roles of publishing a book: writing it, locating and paying for (or trading services for) a content and then a copy editor, locating and paying for (or trading services for) a cover designer and an interior (hard copy and digital) designer, printing, marketing, and finally, distribution.

Because self-publishing, like traditional publishing, can be expensive, I turned to crowdsourcing to fund *The Catalain Book of Secrets*. As a good Midwestern woman who would be embarrassed to ask for help if she was choking let alone to request money from strangers to publish, market, and distribute a book, I found it incredibly painful to put myself out there. But I believed in the book, and I couldn't afford to self-publish on my own.

On October 1, 2014, my Kickstarter campaign went live.

I requested $12,056.

By October 31, 2014, I'd raised $12,671.

I self-published the next month.

Here's what goes into self-publishing:

1. Write book.

2. Revise, fine-tune, and edit book.

3. Hire a professional editor.

4. Either design your own cover or hire a cover designer. Books really are judged by their cover, so if you do not have design skills, I recommend hiring someone who comes highly recommended. Online social media groups like Facebook can help.

5. Either set up your book's interior yourself or hire someone to set it up for you.

6. Send your book out for reviews. Check out Jane Friedman's website (janefriedman.com) for excellent publishing advice, including where self-publishers should go for credible reviews as well as deeper coverage of the self-publishing and traditional publishing basics I'm only touching on here.

7. Upload your book to CreateSpace and Kindle. I've worked with both and found them to be responsive and helpful in the setup stage as well as the royalty-paying stage. They are also both free to use; like an agent, they only make a percentage of what you make. There are other selling options, including Smashwords and Barnes & Noble, but the majority of self-pub sales currently come through Amazon, of which CreateSpace and Kindle are the paperback and e-book arms, respectively.

8. Market your book. Ms. Friedman's website has great details on how to do this, as well.

A caveat. Once your book is out there, whether you snap publish, traditionally publish, or self-publish, there is no taking it back, not now, not in the digital age. Don't let it go until you're ready.

And you don't have to be ready. You do not have to publish that manuscript, ever. The benefits lie in the writing, independent of whether or not you ever publish. If you decide to never send your novel into the sharp world as the wobbly kneed newborn it is, that's just fine. Hang onto it and start writing your next book if you are so inclined.

I don't say this lightly. I was so desperate to get published that I literally cast spells to land an agent, and I'm not even a witch. But who's to say those earth momma candles sprinkled with sage, their wax used to seal my dreams in a Ziploc bag that I slept on for three nights beginning with a full moon, didn't work? But ultimately, the act of writing a powerful, authentic, healing novel is so much more important than publishing it.

Start there.

If you want to get published, you will.

APPENDIXES

APPENDIX A

RECOMMENDED READING

Allende, Isabel. *Eva Luna.*

Allende, Isabel. *The House of the Spirits.*

Cisneros, Sandra. *The House on Mango Street.*

Corbett, David. *The Art of Character: Creating Memorable Characters for Fiction, Film, and TV.*

Friedman, Jane. *Publishing 101: A First-Time Author's Guide to Getting Published, Marketing and Promoting Your Book, and Building a Successful Career.*

King, Stephen. *On Writing: A Memoir of the Craft.*

Lamott, Anne. *Bird by Bird: Some Instructions on Writing and Life.*

Pressfield, Steven. *The War of Art: Break Through the Blocks and Win Your Inner Creative Battles.*

Prose, Francine. *Reading Like a Writer: A Guide for People Who Love Books and for Those Who Want to Write Them.*

APPENDIX B

CHARACTER-BUILDING TABLE

Fill out the following table for each of the three films referred to at end of Chapter 6, "Craft Compelling Characters," entering information as you watch. List the protagonist and antagonist across the top, and, in the boxes below that character, how the qualities listed in the left-hand column were conveyed, including the character's innate humanity. In film, this is called "saving the cat," a crucial opportunity for the viewer or reader to connect with the narrative that is usually demonstrated through a small kindness early in the story.

Some ways that the qualities in the left-hand column are conveyed in film and in novels include gestures, dialogue, clothes, and physical interactions.

Quality/Plot Element	Protagonist's Name:	Antagonist's Name:
HOW THE QUALITY IS CONVEYED		
Character's innate humanity		
Character's strongest personality trait(s)		
Character's main goal		

Quality/Plot Element	Protagonist's Name:	Antagonist's Name:
HOW THE QUALITY IS CONVEYED		
Character's main obstacles		
How other people view this character		
How this character makes you feel about them		
Character's change from the beginning of the film to the end		
Miscellaneous		

APPENDIX C

ESSENTIAL WRITING TERMS

You are probably already familiar with most or all of these terms, so consider this a review. The terms are grouped by focus rather than alphabetized.

Character: A person (usually, though can be an animal or an object) in a narrative

Protagonist: The main character in your novel

Antagonist: The main opposition to the protagonist, usually but not always a person

Character arc: The changes a character (primarily protagonist) undergoes in a narrative

Dialogue: Conversation in writing

Dialogue tags: The section of dialogue indicating who is speaking and how they are speaking. Example:

"Writing is amazing," she said.

In this sentence, "she said" is the dialogue tag.

Point of view or viewpoint: The perspective from which the story is told. If it's first person point of view (often abbreviated POV), the author uses "I" and "me" when writing the main character. Example:

His oily gaze crawled like flies up my body.

You won't see second person point of view ("you") in fiction much. Third person means it's not the first person (me) or the second person (you), but the third person (he/she) through which we experience the story. Example:

His oily gaze crawled like flies up her body.

There are pros and cons to choosing first versus third person when writing your novel and only one hard-and-fast rule: once you choose your POV, you should stick with it, at least in your first book. If you pushed me, I'd advise you to write in first person if you want the easiest route and in third person if you want the most psychic space from what you're writing. Famed writing instructor William Zissner agrees in *On Writing Well* when he writes: "I urge people to write in the first person. . . . Writing is an act of ego and you might as well admit it." (21, 24)

Theme: The unifying or recurring idea in a story. Which theme(s) your book explores will depend on what your protagonist is after. Generally, you don't choose your theme beforehand. It emerges as you write, though I have you begin to consider yours in Chapter 5.

According to Robert Kernen (*Building Better Plots*), there are nine archetypal themes:

- Revenge (*Moby Dick*)
- Betrayal (*Julius Caesar*)
- Catastrophe (*The Handmaid's Tale*)
- Pursuit (*The Fugitive*)
- Rebellion (*Peter Pan*)
- The Quest (*The Mists of Avalon*)

- Ambition (*David Copperfield*)
- Self-Sacrifice (*The Hunger Games*)
- Rivalry (*The Night Circus*)

Verb tense: Verbs are the words that *do*, and tense is when they do them. Present tense means it's happening now. Example:

Her breath <u>is</u> raw from sprinting through the forest.

Extra credit if you noticed that the preceding sentence is written in third person ("Her" is your signal). Here is an example of the same sentence written in third person past tense:

Her breath <u>was</u> raw from sprinting through the forest.

Like point of view, the verb tense you use in writing your book is a personal choice. As long as you are consistent, you'll be fine, though most fiction (with the exception of much young adult) is written in the past tense.

Pacing: The rate at which events unfold in the story

Plot: There's controversy about what constitutes plot versus structure and where to separate character development from plot, but for our purposes, we will define plot as the emotional silhouette of a story. This is unbreakably tied to the sequence of the story's events, but the events are nothing without the emotion they engender. So, going by this definition, the plot of L. Frank Baum's *The Wizard of Oz* is that Dorothy is whisked away from a bleak Kansas farm to a strange land. She is terrified and homesick and must find the great wizard to return home. She encounters trials and makes friends on the way, whereby she learns her strengths and value. When she finally reaches the wizard, he tells her she must kill the Wicked Witch if she wants his help. Dorothy defeats the witch, discovers the wizard is a fraud, and relies on help from her friends to finally return home, completing the final transformation from timid farm girl to brave adventurer.

Scene: The building blocks of plot. A scene is a conflict in a specific place and time. When the place or time changes, the scene is over. A scene can be of any length, though a variety is good.

Setting: The place, time, and mood of the story

Novel: A book-length work of fiction. Note that while the term "novel" always refers to book-length fiction, the generic term "book" can be applied to fiction or nonfiction.

APPENDIX D

NOVEL FORMAT

If you don't plan to publish your book, you don't need to worry about novel format. If you do want to publish, or you want to share your book with others to get feedback or to entertain, plan on typing it in a word processer and making the entire book one document rather than creating a separate file for each chapter. This will save you skies full of time when it comes to editing and printing.

Novel format requires that you begin a new chapter on a fresh page, starting it approximately a third of the way down the page. Center the chapter name and begin typing the text a few lines below that. The entire document should be double-spaced with no extra space between paragraphs. Use 12-point Times New Roman typeface for the main text and include page numbers. Indent at the beginning of each paragraph. If you have a time lapse in your story, as I did in the introduction, use three number signs (###) between paragraphs to indicate the lapse.

Format dialogue like this:

"Jessie sure is good at formatting dialogue!" screamed Jerry.

Ben scratched his chin. "How did she learn?"

"Got me," Jerry said.

Notice that each time someone new speaks, you begin a new paragraph and format accordingly. The punctuation always goes inside the quotation marks (?" not "?). If the piece of dialogue ends in a question mark or an exclamation point, the first word of the dialogue tag that follows is not capitalized unless it's something like a name that would be capitalized anyhow, because the whole unit—dialogue plus dialogue tag—is considered one sentence even when there's punctuation in the middle of it.

If it's inner dialogue (i.e., the character thinks rather than says the words), italicize it:

I erased my mistake and tried again. *Man, this dialogue formatting has a lot of rules.*

Watch for a demonstration of the above formatting rules as you read. You'll see them in most if not all of the novels that you select, with the exception of spacing and typeface, which get a little more complicated when it comes time for a publisher to lay out the book.

APPENDIX E

THE HOUSE ON MANGO STREET SCENE-BY-SCENE OUTLINE

Chapter 7, "Structure Your Story," provided an overview of the plot for Sandra Cisneros' *The House on Mango Street*. The following detailed, scene-by-scene breakdown offers a behind-the-scenes peek at the building blocks of that plot and illustrates, where possible, how Cisneros wove elements from her life into the novel.

Scene Title	Central Conflict	Potential Inspiration
The House on Mango Street	We meet Esperanza and discover what she wants more than anything: a house of her own. The conflict is between her and a nun, who can't believe she lives in a dilapidated house on Mango Street, which makes the reader immediately empathize with her, a child being judged.	Cisneros wrote this vignette as well as "Meme Ortiz" while a graduate student in Iowa struggling with a sense of belonging and the meaning of "home."
Hairs	A scene that mainly provides setting, with a gentle conflict between the types of hair in the family.	In the introduction to the twenty-fifth edition of *The House on Mango Street*, Cisneros writes, "Sometimes I write about people I remember; sometimes I write about people I've just met, often I mix the two together. . . . The people I wrote about were real, for the most part, from here and there, now and then, but sometimes three real people would be braided together into one made-up person." (xxi-xxii)
Boys & Girls	Esperanza can't be alone in her own house because her bedroom door won't close.	
My Name	She doesn't even have her own name; "Esperanza" was her great-grandmother's name first.	
Cathy Queen of Cats	She is judged by a neighborhood girl, worries she won't ever fit in.	
Our Good Day	She loses a friend, steals from her sister.	
Laughter	Her love for the sister from whom she took money is made clear.	
Gil's Furniture Bought & Sold	She can't buy the music box that has enthralled her.	
Meme Ortiz	A crooked house and broken bones.	See "The House on Mango Street" above.
Louie, His Cousin, & His Other Cousin	A stolen car and police chase.	

Scene Title	Central Conflict	Potential Inspiration
Marin	Marin is presented as a girl with big dreams but limited options.	
Those Who Don't	Racism.	
There Was an Old Woman She Had So Many Children She Didn't Know What to Do	A child is hurt, a child no one can be bothered to watch because there are too many of them.	
Alicia Who Sees Mice	A cautionary tale illustrating that even if Esperanza wants to get ahead and go to college, she still may not be able to break free from the neighborhood and the demands of her gender.	See "The Family of Little Feet" below.
Darius & the Clouds	The contradiction between beauty and hope and the grittiness of the neighborhood.	"Darius & the Clouds," "Chanclas," "Minerva Writes Poems," "Geraldo No Last Name," and "The Monkey Garden" were written when Cisneros was a high school teacher in Chicago. She writes of that time, "As a high school teacher, I had no idea how to save my students from their own lives except to include them in my writing, not for their sake, but for my own. I couldn't undo myself from their stories any other way."
And Some More	An argument between friends.	
The Family of Little Feet	Girls explore their burgeoning sexuality and flirt with danger; this is a terrifying scene.	Written after one of Cisneros' Loyola students made a comment about Cisneros' small feet; similarly, "Alicia Who Sees Mice" and "What Wally Said" were inspired by the comments of students she counseled at Loyola.
A Rice Sandwich	Humiliation as Esperanza has to pack a cold rice sandwich to eat with the other kids, is shamed by her mother's note and told she can only join the others this once.	
Chanclas	She has a pretty dress and ugly shoes.	See "Darius & the Clouds" above.

Scene Title	Central Conflict	Potential Inspiration
Hips	The tug between womanhood—getting her hips—and girlhood—playing jump rope with her little sister.	
The First Job	She's sexually assaulted at her first job by the only person who is (initially) kind to her.	See "Red Clowns" below.
Papa Who Wakes Up Tired in the Dark	Her grandfather dies, and she has to step into an adult role.	
Born Bad	Her aunt dies shortly after Esperanza mimics her behind her back.	
Elenita, Cards, Palm, Water	Esperanza is told her future, but it's not what she wants to hear.	
Geraldo No Last Name	An immigrant man is killed and no one cares.	See "Darius & the Clouds" above.
Edna's Ruthie	A child-woman appears in the neighborhood, too fragile for the regular world but not fitting in on Mango Street, either.	
The Earl of Tennessee	A neighbor brings prostitutes home.	
Sire	Esperanza has her first crush on a boy who is trouble.	
Four Skinny Trees	This setting-heavy scene shows a conflict between Esperanza and the world. The stakes begin to rise precipitously from here forward as Esperanza begins her sexual awakening, playing less with the girls and beginning to notice all the trapped women in her neighborhood.	

Scene Title	Central Conflict	Potential Inspiration
No Speak English	A new immigrant woman cannot speak English and is overweight, physically and emotionally trapped in her apartment.	Cisneros' father was born in Mexico City, and the stories of the challenges of his first months in the United States appear throughout.
Rafaela Who Drinks Coconut & Papaya Juice on Tuesdays	A woman who is locked in her house while her husband goes out because he considers her too beautiful to roam free.	
Sally	Esperanza wants to be friends with beautiful Sally but is scared.	
Minerva Writes Poems	A neighbor, who is only a little older than Esperanza but already has two children and likes to write poetry, encourages Esperanza, but is also abused by her husband, showing that writing might not be enough to free Esperanza.	See "Darius & the Clouds" above.
Bums in the Attic	Esperanza fiercely wants her own home, despite and because of what she sees around her.	
Beautiful & Cruel	Esperanza reflects on her powerlessness and begins to claim more space for herself.	
A Smart Cookie	She realizes her mother never claimed her own power and decides she doesn't want to end up like that.	
What Sally Said	Sally gets brutally beaten by her father.	See "The Family of Little Feet" above.
The Monkey Garden	Sally lets boys take her into the garden, hoping one will help her escape her father; Esperanza tries to save her, but Sally doesn't want to be saved. Esperanza realizes she can no longer play the way she used to.	See "Darius & the Clouds" above.

Scene Title	Central Conflict	Potential Inspiration
Red Clowns	Still wanting to trust Sally, Esperanza goes with her to the carnival, where Sally disappears, leaving Esperanza without help when she is sexually assaulted.	In her memoir, Cisneros writes of the struggle to craft this scene. "I felt protective of my protagonist. . . . There was also the difficulty of how to write a story the character didn't want to tell. And how would I write it if I had no firsthand experience either as victim or witness? But then I remembered something that had happened to me in the eighth grade." (28–29) She called on that experience in "The First Job" and that emotion in this vignette.
Linoleum Roses	Sally, still in eighth grade, marries a man so she is no longer trapped with her father; her husband won't let her leave the house.	
The Three Sisters	Three fortune tellers approach Esperanza at a baby's funeral and tell her she's special and must leave Mango Street but also must return.	Cisneros dreamed the first line of this scene while in Athens. She wrote the sentence in her journal and finished the scene and the book on the island of Hydra.
Alicia & I Talking on Edna's Steps	Esperanza elucidates the difference between house and home, but also realizes that if she doesn't help Mango Street, no one will.	
A House of My Own	She finally purchases a house of her own.	In the introduction to the twenty-fifth anniversary of the book, Cisneros writes that she dreamed of having her own house the way other girls dreamed of their weddings.
Mango Says Goodbye Sometimes	She realizes the power of story to quiet the ghosts and to heal those she had to leave behind.	

APPENDIX F

NOVEL OUTLINE TEMPLATE

Week & Deadline	Pyramid on Point Step	Step Requirement	Location of Step	Read	Mark (x) When Done	Miscellaneous Notes	Personal Reward When First Six Steps Are Complete
Week 1 ( )	Steps 1 & 2	Write one-sentence overview, then one-paragraph summary of book	Save in dedicated journal or online file	Read book in the same genre			
Week 2 ( )	Steps 3, 4, & 5	Create character bible, sketch main settings, and freewrite ten minutes each for each sentence in one-paragraph summary	Save in dedicated journal or online file	Read book in the same genre			
Week 3 ( )	Step 6	Outline novel	Outline in table below	Read book in the same genre			
Week 4 ( )	Step 6	Outline novel	Outline in table below	Read book in the same genre			

Week & deadline	Scene/Conflict Personal Experience (If Any) I'm Drawing From	Scene goal/Emotional Outcome/Tone Personal Experience (If Any) I'm Drawing From	Date & Setting	Read Any Fiction (Mark x If Reading That Week)	Word Count When Done	Act	Personal Reward After A Draft Of Each Act Is Completed
Week 5 ( )						**ACT I DEPARTURE** Act I must provide the inciting incident that sets the book in motion, introduces the novel's central conflict, and presents the main characters, showing rather than telling what the protagonist wants more than anything.	
Week 6 ( )							
Week 7 ( )							
Week 8 ( )						(Draw a line after the scene that ends the setup and includes a major obstacle toward the protagonist's forward momentum and thus ends Act I.)	
Week 9 ( )							

Week & deadline	Scene/Conflict Personal Experience (If Any) I'm Drawing From	Scene goal/Emotional Outcome/Tone Personal Experience (If Any) I'm Drawing From	Date & Setting	Read Any Fiction (Mark x If Reading That Week)	Word Count When Done	Act	Personal Reward After A Draft Of Each Act Is Completed
Week 10 ( )						ACT II FULFILLMENT Act II raises the stakes, bringing the protagonist closer to what they want more than anything. (Draw a line after the scene that shows the protagonist just within reach of or having achieved their fulfillment, thus concluding Act II.)	
Week 11 ( )							
Week 12 ( )							
Week 13 ( )							

Week & deadline	Scene/Conflict Personal Experience (If Any) I'm Drawing From	Scene goal/Emotional Outcome/Tone Personal Experience (If Any) I'm Drawing From	Date & Setting	Read Any Fiction (Mark x If Reading That Week)	Word Count When Done	Act	Personal Reward After A Draft Of Each Act Is Completed
Week 14 ( )						ACT III RETURN Act III shows the protagonist realizing or having just realized their main goal and returning to a new life; all loose ends are tied up.	
Week 15 ( )							
Week 16 ( )							
Week 17 ( )							

Week & deadline	Scene/Conflict Personal Experience (If Any) I'm Drawing From	Scene goal/Emotional Outcome/Tone Personal Experience (If Any) I'm Drawing From	Date & Setting	Read Any Fiction (Mark x if Reading That Week)	Word Count When Done	Act	Personal Reward After A Draft Of Each Act Is Completed
Week 18 ( )							
Week 19 ( )							
Week 20 ( )							
Week 21 ( )							
Week 22 ( )							

Week & deadline	Scene/Conflict Personal Experience (If Any) I'm Drawing From	Scene goal/Emotional Outcome/Tone Personal Experience (If Any) I'm Drawing From	Date & Setting	Read Any Fiction (Mark x If Reading That Week)	Word Count When Done	Act	Personal Reward After A Draft Of Each Act Is Completed
Week 23 ( )							
Week 24 ( )							
Week 25 ( )							
Week 26 ( )							
Week 27 ( )							

Week & deadline	Scene/Conflict *Personal Experience (If Any) I'm Drawing From*	Scene goal/Emotional Outcome/Tone *Personal Experience (If Any) I'm Drawing From*	Date & Setting	Read Any Fiction (Mark x If Reading That Week)	Word Count When Done	Act	Personal Reward After A Draft Of Each Act Is Completed
Week 28 ( )							
Week 29 ( )							
Week 30 ( )							
Week 31 ( )							
Week 32 ( )							

Week & deadline	Scene/Conflict Personal Experience (If Any) I'm Drawing From	Scene goal/Emotional Outcome/Tone Personal Experience (If Any) I'm Drawing From	Date & Setting	Read Any Fiction (Mark x If Reading That Week)	Word Count When Done	Act	Personal Reward After A Draft Of Each Act Is Completed
Week 33 ( )							
Week 34 ( )							
Week 35 ( )							
Week 36 ( )							
Week 37 ( )							

Week & deadline	Scene/Conflict Personal Experience (If Any) I'm Drawing From	Scene goal/Emotional Outcome/Tone Personal Experience (If Any) I'm Drawing From	Date & Setting	Read Any Fiction (Mark x If Reading That Week)	Word Count When Done	Act	Personal Reward After A Draft Of Each Act Is Completed
Week 38 ( )							
Week 39 ( )							
Week 40 ( )							
Week 41 ( )							
Week 42 ( )							

Week & deadline	Scene/Conflict Personal Experience (If Any) I'm Drawing From	Scene goal/Emotional Outcome/Tone Personal Experience (If Any) I'm Drawing From	Date & Setting	Read Any Fiction (Mark x If Reading That Week)	Word Count When Done	Act	Personal Reward After A Draft Of Each Act Is Completed
Week 43 ( )							
Week 44 ( )							
Week 45 ( )							
Week 46 ( )							
Week 47 ( )							

Week & deadline	Scene/Conflict Personal Experience (If Any) I'm Drawing From	Scene goal/Emotional Outcome/Tone Personal Experience (If Any) I'm Drawing From	Date & Setting	Read Any Fiction (Mark x if Reading That Week)	Word Count When Done	Act	Personal Reward After A Draft Of Each Act Is Completed
Week 48 ( )							
Week 49 ( )							

Week & Deadline	Pages to Edit	Task(s)	Mark (x) When Done	Miscellaneous Notes	Components of Celebration When Editing Is Complete
Week 50 ( )	First half (page ___–___)	• Opening scene has strong emotional impact • Inciting incident is powerful and makes clear what the protagonist wants more than anything • All characters are introduced • Subplot(s) is introduced • Every scene moves the protagonist closer to what they want more than anything; scenes are interrelated rather than episodic; every scene includes at least one component of ARISE • The organization makes sense • The stakes get higher			
Week 51 ( )	Final half (page ___–___)	• Every scene moves the protagonist closer to what they want more than anything; scenes are interrelated rather than episodic; every scene includes at least one component of ARISE • Stakes get increasingly higher as they get closer to goal • The protagonist ends the book a different person than when the book started • The subplot(s) comes full circle • All loose ends are tied up			
Week 52 ( )	Entire novel	• Spellcheck and then read it out loud, using the line-editing checklist in Chapter 10 as a guide			

Bibliography

CHAPTER 1

Brashares, H. J., & Catanzaro, S. J. (1994). Mood regulation expectancies, coping responses, depression, and sense of burden in female caregivers of Alzheimer's patients. *Journal of Nervous and Mental Disease, 182,* 437–442.

Esterling, B. A., Antoni, M. H., Kumar, M., & Schneiderman, N. (1990). Emotional repression, stress disclosure responses, and Epstein-Barr viral capsid antigen titers. *Psychosomatic Medicine,* 52(4), 397–410.

Greenberg, M. A., Wortman, C. B., & Stone, A. A. (1996). Emotional expression and physical health: Revising traumatic memories or fostering self-regulation? *Journal of Personality and Social Psychology,* 71(3), 588–602.

Klein, K., & Boals, A. (2001). Expressive writing can increase working memory capacity. *Journal of Experimental Psychology: General,* 130, 520–533.

Lepore, S. J., & Greenberg, M. A. (2002). Mending broken hearts: Effects of expressive writing on mood, cognitive processing, social adjustment, and health following a relationship breakup. *Psychology and Health, 17*(5), 547–560.

Lepore, S. J., & Smyth, J. M. (eds.). (2002). *The writing cure: How expressive writing promotes healing and emotional well-being.* Washington, DC: American Psychological Association.

Norman, S. A., Lumley, M. A., Dooley, J. A., et al. (2004). For whom does it work? Moderators of the effects of written emotional disclosure in a randomized trial among women with chronic pelvic pain. *Psychosomatic Medicine, 66*, 174–183.

Petersen, S., Bull, C., Propst, O., Dettinger, S., & Detwiler, L. (2005). Narrative therapy to prevent illness-related stress disorder. *Journal of Counseling and Development, 83*(1), 41–47.

Petrie, K. J., Fontanilla, I., Thomas, M. G., et al. (2004). Effect of written emotional expression on immune function in patients with Human Immunodeficiency Virus infection. A randomized trial. *Psychosomatic Medicine, 66*, 272–275.

Scott, V. B., Robare, R. D., Raines, D. B., et al. (2003). Emotive writing moderates the relationship between mood awareness and athletic performance in collegiate tennis players. *North American Journal of Psychology, 5*, 311–324.

Smyth, J. M., Stone, A. A., Hurewitz, A., & Kell, A. (1999). Effects of writing about stressful experiences on symptom reduction in patients with asthma or rheumatoid arthritis. *Journal of the American Medical Association, 281*, 1304–1329.

Smyth, J. M., True, N., & Souto, J. (2001). Effects of writing about traumatic experiences: The necessity of narrative structuring. *Journal of Social and Clinical Psychology, 20*, 161–172.

Ussher, J. M., Hunter, M., & Cariss, M. (2002). A woman-centred psychological intervention for premenstrual symptoms, drawing on cognitive-behavioural and narrative therapy. *Clinical Psychology and Psychotherapy, 9*(5), 319–331.

Vromans, L. P., & Schweitzer, R. D. (2010). Narrative therapy for adults with major depressive disorder: Improved symptom and interpersonal outcomes. *Psychotherapy Research, 21*(1), 4–15.

Weber, M., Davis, K., & McPhie, L. (2006). Narrative therapy, eating disorders and groups: Enhancing outcomes in rural NSW. *Australian Social Work, 59*(4), 391–405.

CHAPTER 2

Davis, J. (2004). *The journey from the center to the page: Yoga philosophies and practices as muse for authentic writing.* New York: Gotham Books.

Furness, H. (2015, October 20). Internet gives readers 'false sense of entitlement', Joanne Harris says. *The Telegraph.* Retrieved from *http://www.telegraph.co.uk/news/media/11941486/Internet-gives -readers-false-sense-of-entitlement-Joanne-Harris-says*

Goldberg, N. (1986). *Writing Down the Bones: Freeing the Writer Within.* Boston: Shambhala.

Pennebaker, J. W. (1997). *Opening Up: The Healing Power of Expressing Emotions.* New York: Guilford Press.

CHAPTER 3

Berns, G. S., Blaine K., Prietula, M. J., & Pye, B. E. (2013). Short- and long-term effects of a novel on connectivity in the brain. *Brain Connectivity, 3*(6), 590–600. doi: 10.1089/brain.2013.0166

Djikic, M., Oatley, K., & Moldoveanu, M. C. (2013). Opening the closed mind: The effect of exposure to literature on the need for closure. *Creativity Research Journal, 25*(2), 149–154. doi: 10.1080/10400419.2013.783735

Kidd, D. C., & Costano, E. (2013). Reading literary fiction improves theory of mind. *Science, 342*(6156), 377–380. doi: 10.1126/science.1239918

Oatley, K. (1999). Why fiction may be twice as true as fact: Fiction as cognitive and emotional simulation. *Review of General Psychology*, *3*, 101–117.

Wilson, R. S., Boyle, P. A., Yu, L., Barnes, L. L., Schneider, J. A., & Bennett, D. A. (2013). Life-span cognitive activity, neuropathologic burden, and cognitive aging. *Neurology*, *81*(4), 314–321. doi: 10.1212/WNL.0b013e31829c5e8a

CHAPTER 7

Cisneros, S. (2009). *The House on Mango Street* (2nd ed.). New York: Vintage.

Cisneros, S. (2015). *A House of My Own: Stories from My Life*. New York: Alfred A. Knopf.

King, S. (2000). *On Writing: A Memoir of the Craft*. New York: Scribner.

CHAPTER 8

Hosseini, K. (2007). *A Thousand Splendid Suns*. New York: Riverhead Books.

Munoz, L. M. (2014, June 28). What triggers spontaneous memories of emotional events? *Cognitive Neuroscience Society*. Retrieved from *https://www.cogneurosociety.org/spontaneous_memories_weymar/*

Munro, A. (1971). *Lives of Girls and Women*. Toronto: McGraw-Hill Ryerson.

Vermetten, E., & Bremner, J. D. (2003). Olfaction as a traumatic reminder in posttraumatic stress disorder: Case reports and review. *Journal of Clinical Psychiatry*, *64*, 202–207.

CHAPTER 9

Montgomery, D. (2013, February 8). Isabel Allende's 'The House of the Spirits' at GALA Hispanic Theatre. *Washington Post.* Retrieved from *http://www.washingtonpost.com/entertainment /theater_dance/isabel-allendes-the-house-of-the-spirits-at-gala -hispanic-theatre/2013/02/07/409b202e-6ec9-11e2-aa58 -243de81040ba_story.html*

Zinsser, W., editor. (1989). *Paths of Resistance: The Art and Craft of the Political Novel.* Boston: Houghton Mifflin.

CHAPTER 10

Lamott, A. (1994). *Bird by Bird: Some Instructions on Writing and Life.* New York: Pantheon Books.

APPENDIX C

Kennen, R. (1999). *Building Better Plots.* New York: F + W Media.

Zinsser, W. (2001). *On Writing Well: The Classic Guide to Writing Nonfiction* (25th anniversary edition). New York: HarperCollins.

APPENDIX E

Cisneros, S. (2015). *A House of My Own: Stories from My Life.* New York: Alfred A. Knopf.

Acknowledgments

One day, I was sitting in the hippie Unity Spiritual Center in Sartell, Minnesota. On this particular day, a guest minister was delivering the sermon. She began talking about soulmates. She said that Americans have a romantic view of what a soulmate is, our perspectives largely shaped by rom coms, romance novels, and fairy tales. A real soulmate, she said, isn't the knight in shining armor. Oh no. A real soulmate is that person who irritates you into getting off your ass and becoming the person you were meant to be.

She shared that her first soulmate was the guy who made her job as a therapist so unbearable that she was forced to leave the comfort of the familiar. This resulted in her discovering her real life passion: being a minister. Awesome concept, yes? When you look at soulmates in this way, there is inspiration in the buffoon who irks you, holiness in the creep who cheats on you, grace in the boss who micromanages your day. Like rude little cattle prods, these people guide us from where we are to the place we are supposed to be. In honor of this interpretation, I'd like to acknowledge everyone who has ever made my life difficult. It's not easy to be the bad guy—though some of you seemed to relish it more than others—and I am grateful for your help in getting me to this point in my life. I forgive you your trespasses and wish you a hairy soulmate army of your own.

I am also grateful for the more intentional friends in my life: my husband, Tony, who provides me safety, support, and play, which are coincidentally the three legs of the springboard I require to attain new heights. My children, Zoë and Xander, who are the freaking winning lottery tickets of life partners. My agent, Jill, who guided the writing of this book from spark to paperback. Jessica Morrell, my freelance editor, who has the eye of an eagle, the soul of a crone, and the skills of a wizard. My writing tribe, who, when I'm lucky enough to find myself in the same city as them, make me feel like

I'm in the right place at the right time—Jessie II, Terri, Catriona, Linda, Simon, Johnny, Reed, Hank, Dan, Angel, Shannon, Lori, and Hallie. My close friends Christine, Cindy, and Kellie, three beautiful life guides who know how to laugh, drink wine, and get right to the heart of what is important (I know—redundant).

I'm also working with a new crew on this book, the good people at Conari. Thank you to everyone there for giving *Rewrite Your Life* a home, and particularly to Christine LeBlond, whose keen editorial eye brought my best book forward, and Chuck Hutchinson, who copyedits like a dream.

And most especially, thank you to the readers of this book. It takes courage to choose joy, and your evolution makes this world a better place for all of us. Big love.

About the Author

JESSICA LOUREY is best known for her critically-acclaimed Murder-by-Month mysteries and her latest book, *Salem's Cipher,* earned starred reviews from *Library Journal* and *Booklist.* She is a tenured professor of creative writing and sociology, a TEDx presenter, and a sought-after keynote speaker. Jessica also leads healing writing retreats around the country. Visit her at *www.jessicalourey.com.*

CK Photography

Mango Publishing, established in 2014, publishes an eclectic list of books by diverse authors—both new and established voices—on topics ranging from business, personal growth, women's empowerment, LGBTQ studies, health, and spirituality to history, popular culture, time management, decluttering, lifestyle, mental wellness, aging, and sustainable living. We were recently named 2019 and 2020's #1 fastest-growing independent publisher by *Publishers Weekly*. Our success is driven by our main goal, which is to publish high-quality books that will entertain readers as well as make a positive difference in their lives.

Our readers are our most important resource; we value your input, suggestions, and ideas. We'd love to hear from you—after all, we are publishing books for you!

Please stay in touch with us and follow us at:
      Facebook: Mango Publishing
      Twitter: @MangoPublishing
      Instagram: @MangoPublishing
      LinkedIn: Mango Publishing
      Pinterest: Mango Publishing
      Newsletter: mangopublishinggroup.com/newsletter

Join us on Mango's journey to reinvent publishing, one book at a time.